The Really Useful Book of ICT in the Early Years

The inclusion of IC..m reflects the need to encourage forward-l...nd nurseries. This book enables you to help young child...........................nowledge, understanding and skill in the use of ICT, with chapters f...................utors with a wide range of practical experience. Full of ideas and new think...........practical guide shows you how to:

- promote independence in children's use of ICT through resources like digital cameras and role-play toys;
- explore the nature of creativity through ICT, using it to support the more traditional areas of art, music, dance and writing;
- use ICT to enhance the physical and sensory aspects of outdoor learning experiences;
- harness the potential of ICT in reaching children with a variety of different learning needs, particularly those with profound and multiple learning difficulties, or autistic spectrum disorders;
- value children's home experiences of ICT and build on what they already know, and how to work with parents in developing their child's ICT capability.

ICT can underpin all areas of learning for young children; this highly practical, inspirational and informative text is therefore relevant to all practitioners and students training in Early Years education.

Harriet Price works for Cambridgeshire Nursery Centres developing uses of ICT for children and adults within their settings, delivering the Early Years Partnership training in ICT, working as an associate advisor for the ICT service for Cambridgeshire and delivering local and national training in ICT in the Early Years Foundation Stage.

Other titles in the Really Useful series:

The Really Useful Maths Book: A Guide for Primary Teachers
Tony Brown and Henry Liebling

The Really Useful Science Book: A Framework of Knowledge for Primary Teachers,
Third Edition
Steve Farrow

The Really Useful Literacy Book: Being Creative with Literacy in the Primary Classroom,
Second Edition
Tony Martin, Chira Lovat and Glynis Purnell

The Really Useful ICT Book: A Framework of Knowledge for Primary Teachers
Nick Packard and Steve Higgins

The Really Useful Book of ICT in the Early Years

Edited by Harriet Price

Routledge
Taylor & Francis Group

LONDON AND NEW YORK

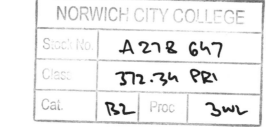

First published 2009
by Routledge
2 Park Square, Milton Park, Abingdon, Oxon OX14 4RN

Simultaneously published in the USA and Canada
by Routledge
270 Madison Ave, New York, NY 10016

Routledge is an imprint of the Taylor & Francis Group, an informa business

© 2009 selection and editorial matter, Harriet Price; individual chapters, the contributors

Typeset in Palatino by
RefineCatch Ltd, Bungay, Suffolk
Printed and bound in Great Britain by
MPG Books Ltd, Bodmin, Cornwall

British Library Cataloguing in Publication Data
A catalogue record for this book is available from the British Library

Library of Congress Cataloging in Publication Data
The really useful book of ICT in the early years / edited by Harriet Price.
    p. cm.
  Includes bibliographical references and index.
  1. Information technology – Study and teaching (Early childhood) – Great Britain.   2. Information
technology – Study and teaching (Elementary) – Great Britain.   3. Elementary school teaching – Great Britain
– Computer network resources.   4. Telecommunication in education – Great Britain.   I. Price, Harriet.
  LB1139.35.C64R43 2009
  372.133'4 – dc22
  2008026412

ISBN10: 0–415–43418–1 (pbk)

ISBN13: 978–0–415–43418–8 (pbk)

Contents

Contributors

Rachel Ager

Rachel started her teaching career in a Reception class and taught in primary schools for 15 years. She currently works for Northamptonshire County Council, where she heads up the Primary ICT Team. She has particular responsibility for developing the use of ICT in the Early Years Foundation Stage and for the last three years half her time has been working on Early Years Foundation Stage ICT, and Northamptonshire has gained national recognition for the model of good practice they have developed in the use of ICT in the Early Years Foundation Stage. She delivers training and seminars in Northamptonshire, nationally and internationally. She has been to Australia twice to speak at conferences and has delivered a seminar at BETT this year.

Julia Coles

Julia is an Early Years Foundation Stage Co-ordinator in a primary special school that caters for children with severe learning difficulties, profound and multiple difficulties and autistic spectrum disorders. She is also the ICT Co-ordinator for the school and has been involved in the NIAS Foundation Stage ICT Strategy since 2003/4 in the role of Lead Foundation Stage ICT Teacher. This role has involved her in supporting colleagues within local mainstream and special schools, offering training and raising expectations of the impact of ICT in the Early Years Foundation Stage classroom.

Sally Dennis

After working as a primary school teacher, special education teacher and early intervention itinerant support worker in Australia, Sally moved to the UK where she has been working for the London Borough of Ealing. Her current role as an ICT project co-ordinator is to lead the development of Early Years ICT borough-wide through projects focused on Listening to Young Children. The role also facilitates the use of ICT as a communication tool for development workers and service teams in support of joined-up working. Sally also works as a researcher for The Engine Room, Wimbledon

School of Art and is currently researching Ealing's 'Creativity Matters' project focused on young children's engagement in creative processes.

Karen James and Chris Cane

Karen is an Early Years advisory teacher in Brent. She works alongside the ICT team, primarily with Chris, who is the ICT consultant with responsibility for Early Years. Together they are developing ICT in the Early Years across both non-maintained and maintained settings. They are both keen that ICT should be used as a tool for learning integrated across the curriculum.

Lynn Kennington and Julie Meaton

Lynn has been head of Gamesley Early Excellence Centre, a designated children's centre, for 20 years. Before this she was a community teacher, nursery teacher and primary teacher. As head Lynn has led the innovative use of ICT in the foundation curriculum for which the centre is nationally renowned.

Julie has worked as a teacher in several nursery schools and has for the last six years been the senior teacher at Gamesley Early Excellence Centre and is now the deputy head of the centre.

The centre was the first Early Years establishment to gain a BECTA award for ICT innovation and change and the first nursery school in the country to gain a NAACE quality mark for ICT. A second BECTA award was gained last year for advice and training in ICT due to the staff's successful training programme nationally and internationally. Julie and Lynn have written several articles for Early Years publications and currently work with BECTA, NAACE, the DfES, Sure Start, the National Primary Strategy, London University and the National College for School Leadership in order to help to spread the word that ICT is very relevant to the lives of young child and can be used as a motivating tool to help children to learn.

Heather Lowe

Heather began her teaching career in the East End of London with primary-aged children. Since moving to Cambridge she developed an interest in the Early Years, and became head of Homerton Children's Centre about 10 years ago. The school was designated as an Early Excellence Centre and an initial enthusiasm for ICT was developed through this. She now delivers training for the EYFS, and in particular ICT, locally and nationally.

Harriet Price

Harriet originally trained at London University, where she completed a B.Ed., specialising in Early Years Education, and an MA in Language and Literature. She worked in inner-city nursery and primary schools in London and then moved to Cambridge, where she continued to teach in nurseries and across the primary age range.

She worked as a learning support teacher with children with physical disabilities where technology was often their primary form of communication. As well as being an ICT co-ordinator, this experience developed her first-hand knowledge of ICT and individual needs and she grew passionate about ICT as a tool for learning.

In 1998 she opened an educational software shop for schools and families. It was the first in the country to have a 'try before you buy' policy where children could play at the computers and try out the software. Even 18-month-olds would bring their families in, clamber up onto the chairs, move the mouse and make things happen! After selling the educational software shop, she went on to deliver ICT training for the New Opportunities Fund, the Care and Education Partnership and for the Cambridgeshire County ICT service.

She now tutors and writes about ICT in the Early Years. She is based in Cambridgeshire children's centres developing their ICT both in the centres and in the universities they serve. Harriet's chapters are based on her experiences at Homerton Children's Centre. The children are her teachers and help her constantly to check the parameters of the benefits and cases of ICT in the Early Years.

Introduction

Harriet Price

ICT, Information and Communications Technology, has a broad meaning within an Early Years setting. It is often easily referred to simply as 'technology'. This is not strictly accurate, as technology includes far more than the electronic technology usually being referred to; however, it is a more user-friendly term. In this book we use the terms 'ICT' and 'technology' interchangeably, the term 'technology' being more readily associated with our own lives and all the equipment we find ourselves surrounded with in our homes, work place and local environment. This book is about the uses of that technology, the technology that surrounds children in their everyday lives.

This book has come together out of best practice in using technology in the Early Years. It falls between academic books on ICT and books that simply give ideas for ICT activities. It is primarily a practical book, but one that aims to give sound reasons for appropriate and relevant ways of using technology in the Early Years. All of the contributing authors have first-hand experience of developing uses of ICT in the Early Years. These uses arise out of our pedagogy; we all expect technology to fit in with the way we believe young children learn and not for the technology to lead us.

The chapters in this book reflect an underlying belief in child-centred education and learning through play. We believe children need to be able to play with technology and explore it freely. This will help them to have a sense of control over the technology, to recognise its uses in the world around them and to gain a sense of empowerment as they take on some of its tools for their own purposes. Children learn both about and through technology. They learn about technology as they investigate what it can do, how it works and what it can be used for, and they learn through technology when they use it as a tool for a purpose: for example, using a camera to take a photograph of something they have made. This book shows how both learning about and learning through technology can add to young children's learning. Technology can add totally new elements to a learning environment; a child taking a video of friends' role play, for example, can lead to ways of reflecting on the play together at a later stage that simply would not be possible without technological tools.

In considering appropriate uses of ICT in the Early Years the contributing authors owe a debt to John and Iram Siraj-Blatchford. Their work on the Developmentally Appropriate Technology for Early Childhood (DATEC) project[1] has influenced all of our practice. Their guidance provides an excellent base for decision-making, both in choosing technologies in the Early Years and in planning uses of technology. Based on the B's 8 key I we can consider the following key identifiers in providing technology in the Early Years:

1. **Applications should be educational**
   We cannot take it for granted that decisions are being made on this premise, but they must be. Technology is furiously marketed these days and great thought and care must be given to selecting technology that supports and enhances children's learning.

2. **Encouraging collaboration**
   How is the technology provided? Are areas around a tape recorder, CD-player or computer inviting for adults and children to sit together? Are children able to combine materials to work effectively together: for example, to add Bee-Bots to play with blocks so that they have a context for shared imagination and problem solving?

3. **Integration and play through ICT**
   Is technology fully embedded? Are children using technological tools for meaning-ful and real purposes? For example, can they use a computer to design and print wrapping paper? Can they take photographs to share with their friends and families? Do children have full access to the technology around them so that they can select tools in their spontaneous play?

4. **The child should be in control**
   Have children been shown how to use the equipment so that they can become independent in their choices and uses? Are children encouraged to talk about tech-nology so they can begin to have a critical sense of the place it holds in their lives?

5. **Applications should be transparent and intuitive**
   Children should be able to manage appropriate technology. Try the technology out with them. Do they find it easy to explore? Can they manage to operate it at some level? Do they readily put it to use?

6. **Applications should not contain violence or stereotyping**
   Conscious judgments need to be made about what we are providing. Images on websites, particularly, should be watched for.

7. **Awareness of health and safety issues**
   Carry out a health and safety audit of all your equipment.

8. **Educational involvement of parents**
   This runs through the entire decision-making process about the uses of technology in the Early Years. See Chapter 9 for ideas on working with parents.

Technology is a challenging area in Early Years practice, not least because of the fast pace at which technology moves within our world today. New technologies bring along with them new ways of learning and we need to keep critical but open minds about these transformations. It is our children who are born into this increasingly tech-nological world and by sharing this technology with them and encouraging a dialogue with them we can hope to develop thoughtful and critical uses of ICT. Children learn skills and knowledge in using ICT and possibly more importantly, build a cultural understanding about its place in their lives. Because of this, the chapters in this book try to reflect both the teaching of skills and knowledge of using ICT *and* developing communication and language around technology. Technology is not viewed in these chapters as something discrete, or an 'add-on' to the learning environment, but as part of a relevant and meaningful learning environment reflecting children's worlds today. In the settings that the authors of these chapters write about, technology is fully embedded, often seeming to disappear in environments that are full of first-hand sensory experiences such as sand, water, clay, blocks, glue, paint, earth, musical instruments, miniature world toys, books, dressing-up clothes, climbing frames and so on. Technology does not need to be flashy or to inhibit a rich play-based environment and we hope that these chapters help to show this and celebrate the advantages that technology can bring to young children's learning.

Note

1   This guidance is written about more fully on the DATEC website, http://www.ioe.ac.uk/cdl/DATEC

1 Integrating ICT into the Early Years curriculum

Lynn Kennington and Julie Meaton

Introduction

The march of information and communications technology is fast and unrelenting. No sooner has one bought the latest TV or mobile phone than another all-singing, all-dancing model is released and the new one is cheaper and the old one is out of date. This rapid change can be daunting for staff in all the phases of education, trying to learn about new equipment and then applying it to the delivery of the curriculum.

We also need to consider, as we move from e-learning (electronic learning) to m-learning (mobile learning), using our small multimedia, multifunction hand-held devices, that desktop computers and computer suites may no longer be relevant and new technology could be more personalised to the learner, certainly within the class-room or in the bag/pocket! Voice controls, sensors and digital interfaces which use touch or eye/ear attachments will be the future for our youngest children.

Computerisation brings the world outside into the home and classroom like never before and our youngest children need adult help to access learning opportunities from these changes in technology.

When it comes to ICT, Early Years practitioners sometimes worry that they do not have the expertise or the necessary equipment or the time to put it into their practice and write it into their policies and planning.

When local authorities send settings 'ICT boxes' of equipment to encourage use, after the initial excitement has died down, the equipment often remains secure in its box, sitting in a cupboard guiltily reminding us that we haven't used it for six months. Why is this? Is it because sometimes it is viewed as a 'bolt-on' to Early Years practice rather than part and parcel of the integrated planning, or because staff ideas have dried up as to its use, or because of lack of confidence with the equipment or lack of time? Perhaps a bit of everything!

Feasey *et al.* (2003) demonstrated that children were very much inspired by the INTEL QXA computer microscopes which were delivered free to every school in 2002 but research showed that the majority of schools had not taken them out of the box. Yet when the researchers encouraged use they found that teachers and children can become 'companion learners' in a learning partnership to discover its potential and possibilities. Teachers do not always have to be the experts, children and adults can learn together and the microscope has a 'wow' factor which clearly motivates children.

Figure 1.1

Educators often underestimate children's experience and confidence with ICT, even in our youngest children. Adams and Brindley (2006) have perceptively pointed out that:

> the model of the passive child sitting mindlessly pressing buttons and being rather superficially entertained by fancy graphics on a screen seemed totally at odds with the ideal of the young child as an empowered, creative and active learner.
>
> (p. xii)

And as John and Iram Siraj-Blatchford (2006) point out:

> in early childhood education the traditional distinction between technology education and educational technology is blurred ... given the rate of technological change it would be a mistake if practitioners were encouraged to emphasise PC operating skills as their most desired outcomes.
>
> (p. 153)

Yet we still hear that 'mouse control' and 'hand–eye co-ordination' is an aim!

There is still a possibility that software on desktop computers is the sole provision in some classrooms. The result is that the technological equipment provided can act as a barrier to developing ICT across the curriculum because its use is limited. There is a plethora of ICT equipment which can be used successfully in the Early Years learning environment and which can be integrated. Having said this, the equipment approach to ICT in teaching and learning is not always the way forward; it can be restrictive because of practitioner confidence and there is also a very real possibility that it will become dated easily.

An approach in using technology across the curriculum which firmly starts with the curriculum, its delivery, the practitioner's knowledge of this curriculum and how children learn is advocated in this chapter.

If we focus on the child's learning experience instead of the equipment, guidance can never be out of date because learning can be applied to any situation or resources if the objectives are clear.

The practitioner's knowledge is crucial to the imaginative application of the curriculum to the learning situation. At our centre we always maintain that the new ideas, or even the good old ideas worked with new technology, bring fresh approaches to learning and motivate children to learn. Children are delighted by new technology! Staff have plenty of ideas! Put the two together and you have a twenty-first-century Early Years Foundation Stage method of curriculum delivery!

As a staff we have received awards and accolades for our innovative use of ICT within the Early Years curriculum, but it is the imagination of the staff and their extensive experience and knowledge as applied through the equipment which has made our success in this area. Not the equipment but our use of it!

Below are examples of the use of two pieces of equipment. First is a simple 'talking tin', inexpensive to buy . . . (found at www.talkingtins.com).

Figure 1.2

These yellow 3-inch-diameter discs are able to record 10 seconds of sound and play back at the press of a button – a simple piece of equipment which records through a digital chip and operates through a battery. A small handbook could be written on ideas of how to use these tins. They help young children to match sound to words and therefore can be used in phonics, number recognition, play, reading, etc.

If we take a more complex piece of equipment – **a computer** – we can use our e-learning credits to buy software to feed into the machine to support mathematics, for example. But take an imaginative play situation like a shop and consider how we can use a computer like a shopkeeper or a travel agent. Children see computers used all the time in the supermarket. How can we mirror this in play?

Use your imagination! Wheel the computer up to the shop and try it out. Put clip-art images or photos relevant to the shop onto the screen. The children can drag and drop the produce they wish to buy. Or at the travel agent's download Internet holiday sites.

Figure 1.3

Planning for integration

By planning for integration we ensure that ICT should be viewed as a tool to support and enhance teaching and learning and not simply as a skill to be learned and an 'add-on' to the curriculum (although being able to handle and operate pieces of ICT equipment is obviously essential). When ICT is used in an imaginative way to deliver the curriculum and is threaded through all Early Learning Goals, stepping stones, topics, themes and play experiences, then the quality of what is taught and learned is further developed and the effectiveness of the learning process is increased.

Practitioners often have a variety of ways of planning the delivery of the curriculum including Hi Scope, Schemas, etc., but two main approaches are often used:

(a) a thematic approach, delivering the curriculum through projects or topics (see Appendix 12 to this book)

or

(b) an approach which is based on the breadth and depth of the Early Years Foundation Stage stepping stones and Early Learning Goals.

Long-, medium- and short-term plans should include and reflect the way in which ICT is to be used to enrich and develop the curriculum.

A practical suggestion is to put an ICT column in the weekly planning sheets to ensure that educators think creatively about how to teach a concept or plan for an experience using technology. We have a variety of equipment and software, some of which is quite inexpensive and we apply our imaginations and sound curriculum knowledge to the situation in hand.

In the long-term plans one can identify which pieces of equipment will be used (see Appendix 13 to this volume). In the medium term this is elaborated upon in greater depth, covering each area of learning) and in the short term activities are planned in depth with more rigour, looking not only at specific activities and differentiation within the activity but also at the way in which the ICT equipment can be differentiated (see Appendix 15 to this volume and also Appendix 14). This approach ensures that from the outset ICT is given a high priority in the whole process of planning teaching and learning for the child. This should provide evidence of a cross-curricular, focused approach to planned ICT within the Early Years curriculum.

As with all planning, practitioners should focus on specific skills to be taught and learnt, knowledge to be gained and understanding to be developed.

All six areas of learning in the Early Years curriculum are covered. The Early Learning Goals and stepping stones for each half term are selected, activities are planned and consideration is given to how ICT can be imaginatively employed to enhance learning in a particular area. ICT can contribute to all areas of learning, and it motivates children to concentrate and persevere. Indeed, using ICT, such as computers, programmable toys and other electronic equipment, engages many children who may not be attracted by other provision.

AREAS OF THE EARLY YEARS FOUNDATION STAGE CURRICULUM

Personal, Social and Emotional Development

One way in which personal, social and emotional (PSE) education is developed is through collaboration, and technology encourages children to cooperate with each other, learn together, be patient, persevere and concentrate. Crook (2003) advocates strongly for collaborative learning and points out that designers develop software to support the solitary learner: 'What designers have failed to recognise is the fact that the practices of private reflection and interrogation that are required to learn on one's own are at first developed through socially organised learning.' Nursery environments are planned around a social context where peer group learning is the norm. Teachers need to plan carefully for social and collaborative development to ensure that a good learning outcome for all is achieved.

For example, by ensuring that there are always two seats by each computer, children are encouraged to share ideas, take turns, problem solve, and cope with some degree of conflict as they each negotiate solutions to problems. Children working together in pairs are more effective in promoting language and problem solving skills than children working individually or in groups.

Iram Siraj-Blatchford also demonstrates in the REPEC research project (Researching Effective Pedagogy in Early Childhood) that sustained shared thinking is especially valuable in term of children's early learning. This specifically was identified as 'sustained verbal interactions that moved forward in keeping with the child's interest and attention' (Siraj-Blatchford *et al.* 2003). This is more likely to be achieved by the presence of an adult to scaffold and support learning. 'The computer should not be a lonely tool, a counter-culture of speed and light, divorced from adult input' (Fine and Thornbury 2006: 34). Whether there is another child or an adult present, it is clear that young children learn more effectively in partnership.

Awareness of their own learning, motivation, and perseverance are other areas of PSE which are developed and supported through the use of ICT.

Play

As Moyles (1989) pointed out, for every aspect of human development and functioning, there is a form of play. This is worth further consideration when planning play for the twenty-first-century classroom.

An essential element of Early Years education is to develop the children's awareness of themselves socially, emotionally and physically through play. Integrating many forms of ICT into imaginative play situations encourages PSE development. The use of closed-circuit television linking play areas, mobile telephones in the form of walkie-talkies, webcams, karaoke machines, dance mats and programmable toys all involve children working together and sharing.

Play reflects life and children's experiences which are rehearsed in the home and in the classroom. The children of today are observing and experiencing a technological revolution on which to base their play. The wooden till in the corner of the shop is no longer relevant; we have bar codes, self-service, credit card machines, etc. Practitioners are challenged by how this can be mirrored in play.

Lesson Plan

Personal, Social and Emotional Development

Early learning goal

Form good relationships with adults and peers.

Stepping stone(s)

Relate and make attachments to members of their group.

Activity

Gather together a group of six children. Talk about each child in turn, naming, describing, likes/dislikes. Tell the children that you are going to make a lotto game and need their help. One at a time, ask a child to follow a positional direction. Ask one child to sit 'on' a chair, ask another to hide 'under' a table, to stand 'beside' a friend, etc.

Let each child have a turn at finding a position and allow each child in the group to take a digital photograph of a child in that position. Take the children to the computer, load up 'Picture Easy' and together select the 'thumbnails' for the lotto game. Print these out, making two copies of each set of six. Laminate both sets and cut round the individual pictures to make the game. (The laminating can be done later by the practitioner and the game played the following day.) (This activity has strong links to Mathematics Early Learning Goal, 'Use everyday words to describe position'.

ICT resources

- digital camera
- computer
- laminator.

ICT levels of differentiation

1. Can identify a camera.
2. Has some idea of a camera's uses.
3. Points camera in correct direction.
4. Looks through view finder/screen.
5. Presses button to take image.
6. Uses menu to view previous images.

Figure 1.4

Communication, Language and Literacy

Communication, Language and Literacy is also supported very ably by the use of ICT. Multi-link headphones, digital cameras, webcams, CCTV cameras, tape recorders, walkie-talkies, telephones, etc. all encourage the development of speaking and listening skills. The imaginative use of the scanner and photocopier enables practitioners to reduce illustrations from books so that children can retell stories by cutting out the pictures and sequencing the story themselves. Retelling stories using puppets and videoing this to be shown to a large group at story time enables children to develop their speaking skills and increases self-esteem. An interactive whiteboard or smart board can be used to develop writing skills on a large scale (this is particularly important for boys) and can also be used to project videos and photos of the children for circle time.

Webcams, camcorders, karaoke, talking tins, cassette recorders are all about projecting and recording voices which increase speaking confidence and encourage listening.

Figure 1.5

Figure 1.6

Lesson Plan

Communication, Language and Literacy

Early learning goal

1. Retells narrative drawing on language patterns of stories.
2. Speaks clearly and audibly showing awareness of the listener.

Development matters

1. Takes turns in conversations.
2. Talks confidently in a group or to an audience.
3. Develops a simple narrative with clarity and logic.

Activity

Encourage the children to make puppets of a familiar story and use the puppets to retell the story in a puppet theatre. Help a child to record the performance with the camcorder and use the recording in circle time for further discussion.

Extension

Make the puppets by scanning the characters in the book, laminating and attaching them to wooden sticks. The children can help to scan and laminate the pictures.

ICT resources

- camcorder
- television and recorder/or whiteboard and computer
- scanner
- laminator.

ICT levels of differentiation for the camcorder

1. Can identify the camcorder.
2. Switches the camcorder on/off (aided/unaided).
3. Uses 'pause' button.
4. Uses 'rewind' and 'view' facility.

Problem Solving, Reasoning and Numeracy

Excitement is injected into mathematics through imaginative use of ICT. Programmable toys help with many aspects of maths, from number recognition, counting forwards/ backwards, 1:1 correspondence and logic and problem solving skills. Metal detectors are very motivating for children because they introduce the element of surprise and discovery and therefore can be employed for more than finding metal. They can be used to hunt for numbers, shapes and sizes of objects to which metal has been attached.

Of particular note is the small simple robot (Pixie, Romer, Beebot, etc.) for mathematics in the Early Years. Fine and Thornbury (2006) point out that it has a distinctive role and is unique in Early Years education in that it presents an opportunity for children to develop the abstraction of mathematical concepts – from action to representation. The robot is a transitional object which can be whatever the child wishes it to be. It is an innovative and exciting mathematical tool of which every Early Years setting should make maximum use.

Figure 1.7

Remote controlled vehicles may be used outside to develop positional and directional language as children are encouraged to 'drive' their vehicle 'under' the bridge, 'through' the tunnel, 'round' the cone and to stop 'next to' the number 3, etc. Size grading and scanning different sized leaves, making lotto games of shapes and patterns from the environment all help to personalise learning for the child.

Lesson Plan

PSRN

Early learning goal

Use language such as 'circle' or 'bigger' to describe the shape and size of solids and flat shapes.

Development matters

Begin to use mathematical names for 'flat' two-dimensional shapes.

Activity

Children to find piece of metal hidden under laminated shapes using a metal detector.

Laminate six plain shapes. Hide a metal washer underneath one of the shapes and ask the child to 'wave' the hand-held detector over the shapes in turn in order to locate the metal. When the detector sounds, the child names and describes the shape. (This activity can be used to name and describe numbers, letters, animals, etc.)

ICT resources

- metal detector
- laminated shapes.

ICT levels of differentiation

1. Knows what a metal detector is called.
2. Switches detector 'on'/'off'.
3. Knows purpose of metal detector.
4. Knows that when buzzer sounds the object is metal.

Knowledge and Understanding of the World

It is probably the link between ICT and Knowledge and Understanding of the World which is recognised by most people. The Foundation Stage curriculum expects that children can 'Find out about and identify the uses of every day technology and use information and communication technology and programmable toys to support their learning' (Curriculum Guidance for the Foundation Stage, QCA 2000).

It is appropriate, therefore, to acknowledge and recognise that the teaching of ICT skills is important to enable children to have mastery and control over the equipment, in order to facilitate their learning in each curriculum area.

Hand-in-hand with this approach, it is also important to plan for the structured development of ICT skills. This can be differentiated and be progressive. This is easily done by employing a 'rolling program' over each half term, based on the ICT 'stepping stones' for the Foundation Stage curriculum. Each week a skill or piece of equipment is focused upon and differentiated in order to develop competency within this area (see Appendix 16 to this book).

Below is a table of skill differentiation, which can be applied to 14 pieces of equipment and the Internet.

Table 1.1

	Levels of differentiation
Microscope	1. To be able to name the microscope and to know what it is for 2. To place objects to be magnified into correct position 3. To operate the microscope changing settings and to take still photograph
Digital cameras	1. To know name of 2. To take photograph 3. To print out from computer
Video conferencing	1. To have opportunity to communicate with others using this system 2. To name parts and to know that CCTV provides a link between location 3. To pass information to others and to communicate
Pixie/Beebot	1. To be able to switch on/off 2. To be able to move Pixie randomly 3. To be able to program forwards/backwards 4. To be able to program forwards/turn/return
Remote controlled vehicles	1. To be able to switch on/off 2. To be able to move Pixie randomly 3. To be able to make toy move along set route
Software programs	1. To be able to complete program with support 2. To ask for specific software title 3. To be able to complete program unaided 4. To load own disc and print out if appropriate

continued overleaf

	Levels of differentiation continued
Walkie-talkies	1. To know that they enable communication 2. To be able to operate the controls – aided/unaided 3. To hold conversation with others
Webcams	1. To know name of 2. To take photograph/video 3. To communicate with others in various settings
Metal detectors	1. To know name of 2. To operate correctly 3. To know that it finds objects made of metal
Computers	1. To have opportunity to access computer via touch-screen mouse, interactive whiteboard 2. To name peripherals – mouse, monitor, keyboard, printer, webcam, scanner, cursor 3. To use touch screen to select icons, etc. 4. To use mouse to move cursor – select icons (click) (click and drag) (click, drag, drop)
Internet	1. To know it is where we can find information 2. To use some language connected to Internet, e.g. website, downloading, etc. 3. To print picture/photograph from a site
Talking tins	1. To press button and listen to message 2. To press button, listen to message and follow instruction 3. To record message unaided
Cassette recorder	1. To be able to switch on/off 2. To be able to load tape/cassette 3. To be able to rewind, record and play and use associated language
Scanner	1. To be able to switch on/off 2. To name 'scanner' and to know that it copies pictures/work 3. To be able to follow instructions (with help) in order to scan work
Photocopier	1. To be able to switch on/off 2. To name 'photocopier' and to know it copies pictures/work 3. To be able to operate copier by selecting number of copies, size of copy and to press appropriate key to copy

When selecting learning activities which involve a piece of technical equipment, it is important to ask three questions:

1. What has the child gained in terms of knowledge, skill or understanding?
2. Have the learning activities helped the child achieve something they might not have done in any other way through the use of ICT?
3. Will the equipment motivate the child to learn and have fun while learning?

Mapping is encouraged through the use of programmable toys. Looking closely at similarities, differences, patterns and changes can be aided through the use of well-chosen computer programs and the digital microscope. The webcam is marvellous for its applications of time lapse to capture the emergence of a butterfly from its cocoon.

Dismantling pieces of electrical equipment encourages children to enquire and find out about how things work and this helps to improve the child's use of technological language.

Figure 1.8

Lesson Plan

Knowledge and Understanding of the World

Early learning goal

- Look closely at similarities, differences, patterns and change.
- Recognises numerals 1–9.

Development matters

- Talk about what is seen and what is happening.
- Notice and comment on pattern.
- Show an awareness of change.
- Recognise numerals of personal significance.

Activity: To teach an understanding of the life cycle of a frog

Make a simple linear grid (sized according to the length of the Pixie) with numbers 0–10 written in order alongside each Pixie-length box. Place some bubble wrap (frog spawn), model tadpoles, froglets and frogs along the number line. Ask the child to programme the Pixie/Beebot along the line to collect the objects in order of the cycle. Encourage the child either to count the number of Pixie lengths to the item or to 'read' the adjacent number.

Extension

Use a grid where children have to incorporate 'turns' into the program.

ICT resources

- Pixie, Beebot, other programmable toy
- grid
- life-cycle objects.

Figure 1.9

ICT levels of differentiation

1. Switches toy on/off.
2. Explores Pixie randomly.
3. Programs along a line (simple aided/unaided).
4. Completes program, forwards and backwards.
5. Completes complex program.

Physical Development

Physical development, especially the development of fine motor skills, is improved through the child's use and manipulation of ICT equipment: for example, using a mouse and controlling the cursor is quite a high-level skill and it is helpful if the smaller size of mouse is purchased for children.

ICT can be incorporated into many aspects of physical and outdoor play. Metal detectors, walkie-talkies, CD players, remote controlled cars can all be used outdoors. Talking tins are especially good for treasure hunts and for obstacle courses outdoors.

Digital stop watches and heart rate monitors help children to see the effect of exercise on their bodies.

The digital camera can be used to record children's physical challenges, progress and achievements. The resulting photos can be used in assessment files and/or discussed with the children at circle time to build self-esteem and demonstrate ideas and possibilities to others.

Figure 1.10

Figure 1.11

Lesson Plan

Physical Development

Early learning goal

Travel around, under, over and through balancing and climbing equipment.

Stepping stones

- Combine and repeat a range of movements.
- Sit up, stand up, and balance on various parts of the body.

Activity

Set up an obstacle course outdoors. Record an instruction on each tin telling the children what to do, e.g., 'hop five times', 'crawl through the tunnel', 'jump through the hoops', etc. As the child reaches the next obstacle they press the button and listen to the instruction.

Extension

Children to record their own instructions for others to follow.

ICT resources

talking tins.

ICT levels of differentiation for talking tins

1. Presses button.
2. Presses button and listens to and follows instruction.
3. Records own instruction by pressing two buttons and talking into the tin.

Creative Development

Children's creative development can be fostered through a number of pieces of ICT equipment. The overhead projector can be used for silhouette puppet shows and to help children create on a large scale. The digital microscope is an excellent resource for looking closely at and exploring texture. Scanning various shades of colour from the nursery garden in order to create a colour palette from which children can mix their own shades and tints is particularly effective. The use of the karaoke machine, dance mats and electronic keyboards all foster musical development and a music recording studio can be created using this equipment and disco lights and fabrics.

Marsh (2006) demonstrated that children are able to be creative with digital animated films if they are given appropriate resources and support.

Our work in this area has been very exciting and we have produced short animated sequences or clips using a webcam and Duplo figures and blocks. Webcams have several features which enable children and adults to do this easily. The software company 2Simple also produce excellent software, 2Animate, which makes this process easy.

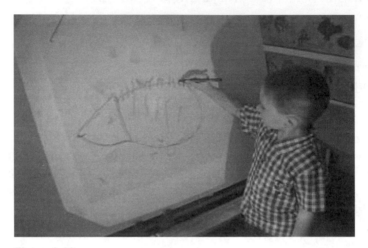

Figure 1.12

Figure 1.13

Figure 1.14

Figure 1.15

Lesson Plan

Creative Development

Early learning goal

Explore colour, texture, shape, form and space in two or thee dimensions.

Stepping stones

Work creatively on a large or small scale.

Activity

The children look at a video clip of dinosaurs on the laptop. They then draw a picture of their favourite dinosaur onto acetate, and use the OHP to project this up onto the whiteboard. Children draw over projected image in order to enlarge their original drawing (creating size to pictures). Children then paint with various shades of textured paint.

ICT resources

- laptop
- overhead projector.

ICT levels of differentiation

1. Switch on/off.
2. Can identify projector.
3. Begins to understand the concept of mirror effect.
4. Begins to understand the concept of size and magnification.
5. Uses the appropriate technological language.

Inclusion

ICT provides the opportunity for all children to access the curriculum. It has the potential for being finely differentiated and for providing individualised, sensitive feedback; therefore it can be particularly effective in helping to close the opportunity gap for children with additional support needs.

Specially designed equipment such as touch screens, switches and appropriate software enable such access. The use of ICT applications to enable children who do not speak to access the whole curriculum can be achieved through visual aids created by staff, shared with parents and used at home and nursery. Visual timetables and social story books are a wonderful way to aid communication.

Children identified as being gifted and talented can benefit hugely from the opportunities ICT has to offer. The use of the Internet to support learning is a fabulous resource to extend the interests of our most able children. There are many excellent programs which have been written to support all curriculum areas and to extend the most able pupil. It is important that children's use of ICT is especially encouraged so that their motivation and capabilities are developed. Gifted and talented children who are more confident can develop their own skills and understanding through supporting and guiding their peers.

Parental partnership

Involving parents in ICT is very rewarding: we have had great success in encouraging fathers, especially, to video their children playing and editing the work. This helps parents to understand the value of play and increases knowledge of their own children's play experiences and how they learn.

Figure 1.16

Figure 1.17

Practitioners are often unable to develop their ideas in delivering the curriculum with technology because an adult is needed to support learning and use the equipment safely. There are no opportunities to give a group of children this attention in a busy classroom – this is especially true of reception classrooms. Using camcorders, webcams, digital microscopes and working with animation all need adult support, which can be found in parent helpers.

It is possible to create videos/DVDs of the staff reading stories, which the children can take home. We have made a listening library which consists of 20 cassette recorders, well-loved story books and cassettes of our voices reading stories. These are lent out to families so that children can listen to stories whenever they wish.

We have recorded the children singing all our favourite nursery rhymes in the nursery and we take each new child a CD on the first home visit so that they can listen to and learn our songs.

There is a lot of potential in communicating with parents with information and communications technology. It is said that a picture conveys more than a thousand words and we have at our disposal the opportunity to take photos, record DVDs, CDs, use closed-circuit TVs, and much more.

Conclusion

1. It is important when integrating ICT across the Early Years Foundation Stage curriculum that practitioners start with a simple piece of equipment and involve all the staff in thinking of activities for its use across the whole curriculum.
2. Encourage children to collaborate in learning situations involving ICT.
3. Take one step at a time and do not worry too much about the 'skills' involved; concentrate on the learning process and the objectives.
4. When staff confidence grows, add ICT in planning columns.
5. Do not be afraid to experiment. Be innovative.
6. Finally, working with technology is fun for adult and child. They can learn about the equipment together, so please remember that everyone should enjoy themselves . . . we all learn better that way!

2 Children's independence and ICT

Heather Lowe

Introduction

'Oh, I *did* it!' A huge grin lit up the face of four-year-old Ben who had just managed to take a digital photograph of his friend playing in the garden. He had been sensitively supported by the adult who enabled him to use the camera independently and play back the image so that both children could see instantly what had been recorded.

The video clip that captured this scene reminded me of why we value children's independence in using technology so much. The journey that the nursery school had taken to arrive at this particular point was a long one, provoking much discussion and thought among the staff.

Our staff have high but realistic expectations of what three- and four-year-olds can achieve and provide activities that build on previous experience, interests and knowledge. We also like to give challenges in which children will have to struggle a little!

Our belief in developing children's independence to its full potential underpins this philosophy. Three-year-olds can generally express themselves fairly clearly, their memories are developing and they are becoming adept at solving everyday problems. Ben, the child I described using the digital camera, was becoming much more aware of his own independence and was really valuing it.

Independence allows us to do what we want and to do it in our own way. This makes us take responsibility for our own actions. It is wonderful to see the gradual realisation when the child understands they are beginning to have control over their learning. With this understanding comes the involvement in decision making, thinking about choices to be made. The staff quickly get to know each individual child, their skills, strengths and level of development so that they can plan accordingly. They aim to develop self-esteem to a high level so that children have the confidence and motivation to see themselves as independent learners.

Quite a few years ago we introduced ICT into the school, as technology became an increasingly important part of the children's worlds. As with any other area of the curriculum, we made it relevant, meaningful and totally hands-on so that children could be in control of their own learning. Our high expectations of independent use just carried on into another exciting area of learning.

As our own confidence and expertise in ICT grew, we gradually began delivering training to practitioners in playgroups, day nurseries, pre-schools and reception classes. However, it quickly became apparent that some people perceived barriers to using technology independently. Here are some of the concerns:

- Three- and four-year-old children are too young to be able to use, understand and operate technology.
- ICT equipment is too expensive and children may possibly break it easily.
- Adults should be in control of ICT resources, which should be stored away and brought out on 'special' occasions.
- Foundation Stage children should only play with traditional resources, e.g., sand, water, blocks.
- Some practitioners have a reluctance and lack of confidence in themselves to use ICT.

I am going to describe how we have incorporated ICT into our learning at Homerton Children's Centre, enabling us all to become independent users, and how we have overcome some of these barriers.

Planning the learning environment

The Centre has worked hard developing children's independence through the physical arrangement of the rooms, outside area and access to resources, and through adults acting as role models.

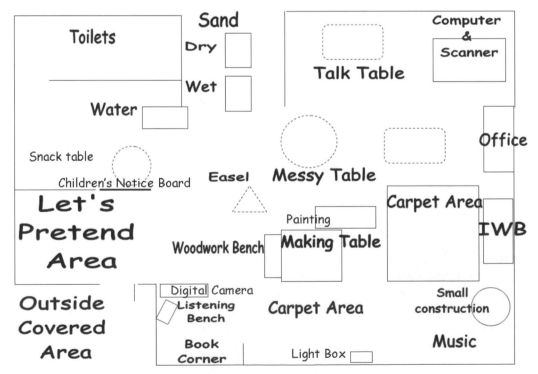

Figure 2.1 A room layout shows how the arrangement of a space can aid independence

The rooms are organised into areas, and class teams plan together based on their observations of the children, the children's interests and needs and differing levels of ability. Some areas are resourced by staff and some by the children. A typical week would look something like the plan shown in Figure 2.2.

Plan of South Room showing Learning Intentions for each area

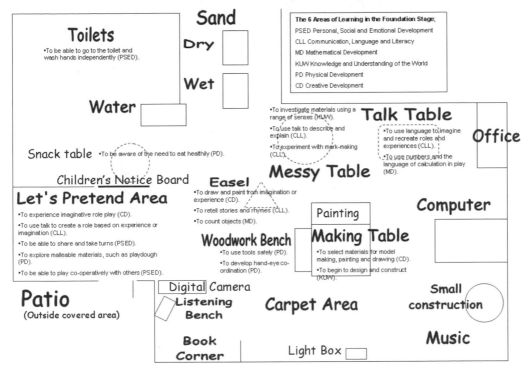

Figure 2.2 Room layout with learning intentions taken from the planning

ICT can be used to help resource an area to support independence. Photographs show the children what the resource is and where to return it to once they have finished with it. (See Figure 2.3).

The following ICT resources are out on a permanent basis and provide continuous provision for children to choose and play with independently and to incorporate into other areas of learning:

- everyday technology or role-play toys (I'd put this at the top of your list)
- computer and printer/scanner
- webcam and microphone
- carefully chosen software
- Internet access
- interactive whiteboard
- digital camera
- digital movie maker
- talking photo albums and cards
- metal detectors
- programmable toys and remote controls

Figure 2.3

- cassette recorder
- CD player.

The children can also access the office photocopier and laminator, and use the microwave, blender and bread maker in their cooking with adult support. Sometimes we plan the use of other equipment to develop children's play and learning:

- overhead projector
- light box
- digital microscope
- laptop for role play
- planned use of software
- remote control vehicles and bugs
- tablet computer
- visualiser.

As you can see, we think that ICT is 'More than just computers' (John Siraj-Blatchford 2002). By playing with a range of technology children can discover the place and purpose of this in their everyday lives. For example, 'Why does the machine go beep when the person passes our shopping through it?' 'What happens when the food goes into the microwave?' 'What does the doctor do on the computer when I go to see him?'

I will explain a little more about these resources and how we see them supporting children's understanding and independence.

Computer and printer

Children may have a computer at home. They may see adults operating PCs in banks, in mummy's or daddy's office, on TV . . . However children must feel comfortable and safe and be allowed maximum independence to further their learning. Imagine if you sat at your desk, head thrust back in order to see the monitor, feet dangling, and hands barely able to hold a giant mouse! It's worth spending time and a little effort to put things right.

Ask yourself the following questions as you observe a child sitting at a computer:

- Are the child's eyes level with the monitor? If not, can you adjust the height of the chair or monitor?
- Are they sitting at a comfortable distance from the monitor? Not too close or too far away.
- Are their feet firmly on the floor? If not, perhaps a block could be used.
- Is the chair the correct size? There are companies who sell children's computer chairs that are not on castors. (To avoid whizzing around the room!)
- Is the mouse child-sized? Using an adult-sized mouse will not be comfortable and will not help independence.
- Can children with additional needs access the computer? Switches which are operated with pressure from the whole of the hand may be easier to use than the relatively fine motor control of a mouse. Or you may like to consider tracker balls.
- Is the keyboard child friendly? There are several styles of keyboards that have large clear lower case letters. Some have a thin skin that prevents sand from dropping inside. Look for those that have all the relevant keys, as some more able children become interested in punctuation or in looking at and experimenting with different symbols.
- Is the software appropriate? Some software is 'transparent', easy to understand how to use, while some is more 'awkward' to interact with and might not be appropriate for a setting. Some software is designed for toddlers and does not require mouse skills.
- Are adults using correct computer vocabulary so that children have the language to ask for help when it is needed?

monitor	keyboard	mouse	computer
cursor	icon	click	drag

A useful addition is a sand timer. Children can be shown how to use this so that they can independently negotiate turns with each other, 'Oh, the sand's gone down – it's my turn now!' This is helpful if you think that a child is spending too long there.

With these small adaptations children can maximise their independence and may not have to ask for adult support so much.

We view the computer as a tool to support learning and prefer it to have a place in the classroom rather than in a remote computer suite in another part of the building. Here is a good example of a child's independent use of the computer.

> We had been talking about Kings and Queens and Jenny, a three-year-old, had become very interested in castles. She had spent a long time on the carpet area building a castle from sturdy wooden blocks. When this construction was finished she went to the computer and self selected a My World program from the front screen. This particular piece of software enables children to choose various buildings and road layouts to design towns and villages. But Jenny selected churches and blocks of flats, clicking and dragging them on top of each other to design a very tall, grand looking castle, which she then printed and proudly showed to her key worker.

Jenny's understanding and development of language in this area of learning was quite remarkable. The staff had also observed and recorded that her independent use of the computer had allowed Jenny to generalise her learning very well.

Rather than selecting one program at a time that is chosen for the children each day, it is better to display an appropriate range of programs that the children can access at their own level of understanding and development. In order that they don't access all areas of the computer, it is essential that it has some kind of protection installed. For example, 'Childlock' ensures that the screen looks exactly the same but the right click on the mouse cannot be used.

Our practitioners have spent a great deal of time looking at software which is suitable for three- and four-year-olds, that avoids stereotyping, is without gender or cultural bias and is open ended, allowing for children's creativity. We install a 'core bank' of software on our machines but only put a few shortcuts to programs on our desktops. These are changed over a period of time, allowing the children to build up their knowledge and confidence of a range of software. By selecting and adding shortcuts to the desktop, staff can plan in the software that is most appropriate for the children's play and learning at that time, and allow the children choice without providing an overwhelming selection.

Core software

Milly's Mouse Skills	Choose and Tell – Nursery Rhymes
Beep!	2Simple IVT
Musical Leaps and Bounds	2Simple City
Leaps and Bounds 3	2Maths City
Revelation Natural Art	2Publish+
2Paint a Picture	2Create a Story
Millie's Maths House	Tizzy's First Tools
Music Toolkit	
	See Appendix 1 Software and resources

We also add role-play software to laptops that we can set up alongside children's role play, and use software to support peripheral hardware such as webcam software that will capture still and moving images and digital camera and microscope software. We try to be strict in not purchasing too much software as having a restricted amount allows all the staff and children to get to know the programs well so that they are able to choose an appropriate program according to children's play, interests and purposes (see Figure 2.4).

Figure 2.4

Another thing to consider is the printer. Printing out a piece of art work in 2Simple or the fantastic bug that has been designed in Millie's Maths House can give children an enormous feeling of self-satisfaction. They will quickly become familiar with the printer icon and will recognise text boxes asking them if they want to print. If you don't want your ink cartridges and reams of paper to be used up, you could adjust the settings to stop printing. Most educational software has this option – look at the teacher options in the software to see what is available. Printing can then become more purposeful when linked with meaningful experiences away from the computer: designing a pattern in 2Paint a Picture for using as wrapping paper, printing envelopes, notices and signs for role play or printing photographs to add to their 'special books' (books to take to and from home to celebrate their achievements).

It is also well worth considering the use of laptops in different areas of the room to enable a meaningful and independent use of a computer, for example, in role-play areas. When we developed a doctor's surgery with the children, we introduced a laptop with At the Doctors program loaded onto it in the 'reception' area. Following adult modelling, the play there became very involved and imaginative as it replicated a real-life situation with the use of meaningful technology. Adding in other technology, such as an overhead projector for looking at x-rays, developed the play still further.

Interactive whiteboard

It is equally important to look at the physical set-up of your interactive whiteboard to enable children to use it as independently as possible.

For small children the whiteboard must be as low as possible, and it is worth insisting on a height that Early Years Foundation Stage children can access easily. Steps in front of the screen may be an option, but safety must be taken into account.

Figure 2.5

One of the joys of whiteboards is their sheer size and the children's ability to make large motor movements in a paint program (e.g. Revelation Natural Art), or a group of children able to join in with dancing (e.g. Musical Leaps and Bounds), or the delight when a child recognises themselves on a slideshow of photographs. The interaction with programs, as children are able to drag objects around the screen with their hands, is of great benefit to children, particularly those with additional needs.

We find that cooperative play can be maximised here and the use of timers or names on a turn-taking board will enable the children to manage this, independent of adult intervention.

Digital cameras

Digital cameras are one of the easiest ways to enhance children's self-esteem and independence and, although we were initially a little nervous about having a camera out all the time for children to access, our fears were unfounded. Staff were concerned that children might:

- drop the cameras;
- damage them with sand, water or messy play resources;
- not understand or be able to operate the camera.

However, the three problems have not arisen and the only damage we have experienced was when a well-meaning mum dropped the camera on a parents' evening!

When choosing a camera, look for:

- a good size and shape for small children to hold;
- one with (or purchase separately) a sturdy neckband that we insist children wear when they use the camera;
- a good size of display;
- buttons that are clear and easy to operate.

The cameras were gradually introduced to the children through structured teaching regarding operation and care. As these principles were understood very quickly, the staff were able to leave the cameras on low, accessible tables. There are visual prompts on how to use the cameras.

Webcams and a digital movie-maker camera

Webcams are particularly cheap ways of enabling children to take digital still and moving images. Their disadvantage is that they are attached to the computer, unless you invest in a wireless webcam, which will be a similar price to the digital movie maker. One option is to buy an extension lead for the attachment of a webcam to the computer. This gives the children a very long lead from the computer, where they'll be able to have greater scope to take photos and video of other experiences around the room, for example, to take a photo of a model they have made to take home or to take video of role play to share with their friends at group time.

The digital movie maker can be detached from its base and taken around with the child. At Homerton the children take these outside and particularly like filming their friends at play. This puts them in the position of being an observer of their peers and helps them to reflect on their own play and learning.

We have been amazed at the children's independent use of the cameras, and how most of them, by the end of their nursery year, are competently switching on the cameras, taking a photograph, attaching the camera to the lead in the computer and printing from it. Other children have been interested in extending their learning and can operate the 'Review' and 'Delete' functions and can scroll through their images.

It is also fascinating to see a child's view of the world. When staff have viewed the disks it is evident which friendships, different areas of the nursery and patterns in the environment are important to a young child. As a digital camera is so portable, it is a useful piece of technology to use in the outdoor learning environment.

Children with additional needs have particularly benefited from using digital cameras, as images of themselves and of their key worker are useful for promoting communication and attention skills.

Programmable toys

The programmable toys are usually kept on a low bench next to the carpet area so that children can access them easily and use them in their play. They are put there after a gradual introduction to the children through focused activities, and then their play and exploration of programmable toys is observed and monitored. Through this process of independent use we have seen that children really begin to understand the basics of programming and by the end of the year some children can perform fairly complex manoeuvres with the toys.

We have used Pixies for quite a long time, but recently we have introduced Beebots and have had a lot of success with these.

The merits of Pixies and Beebots are well worth comparing. See Table 2.1.

Table 2.1

Pixie	Beebot
Looks like a plain metal box but in fact is very open-ended for imaginative play, as staff or children can make paper jackets in any design they like.	Looks like a brightly coloured plastic bug. Has clip-on plastic jackets but still looks like a bug!
You can attach laminated photographs on the front (perhaps a photo of the child) so that they can go on a 'journey' with Pixie.	The round shape makes it less easy to fix photographs onto, but they do have a hook on the back which makes it easy to attach trailers.
Pixie must not be pushed along the floor (doesn't have a gear).	Beebot can be pushed along without harm as it has a gear mechanism.
Pixie can be sent back to the manufacturer for repair.	Once broken, Beebot cannot easily be mended.
Pixie is too susceptible to damage to take outdoors.	Beebot can be taken out doors if used on mats.
Quite expensive – approximately £120.	Relatively cheap – approximately £30.

Both toys have various accessories which may be purchased separately and provide more opportunities for programming, e.g. a football pitch, an obstacle course or plain grids that can be endlessly adapted.

Children with additional needs often understand the use of programmable toys quite well, especially if they are allowed to explore the toy independently without any preconceived notion of outcomes. By pressing buttons they are rewarded with instant results.

Cassette recorders and CD players

Children will often have access to cassette recorders and CD players at home or will have seen adults operating them. When children are shown how to use tapes and CDs, they will be able to have control over their own listening and choose from a range of stories, rhymes and music. If headphones are provided, they can create a private space into which to retreat, and where listening skills are practised and extended.

CDs with pictures, symbols and simple words on the cover can be offered as a choice. Some children love to listen to the same traditional tale over and over again. Some like to follow the story in the book and listen for the bleep asking them to turn the page. Other children can be heard to sing along with favourite rhymes, loudly and oblivious to all that's going on around them.

Practitioners who have visited the nursery have said that they were worried about the children pressing the wrong button and accidentally erasing the tape. We have found that by labelling the 'Start' button with a green sticker and the 'Stop' button with a red sticker, we have largely overcome this problem. It reminds us that children do need to be taught the skills of using tools in their learning. Adults need to model uses and scaffold children's learning for children to be able to use technology competently on their own.

The children take it in turns to wear the Homerton Owl badge, which gives them special responsibilities for the day. At 'tidy-up' time the Homerton Owl is asked to put on a CD. The music is the signal for the children to start putting away the resources ready for group time. The choice of music is limited so that there is a calm selection to influence the atmosphere in the room. This system does seem to stop children marching around shouting 'Tidy-up time, tidy-up time', and doing very little else. When parents are tearing their hair out as their children leave a trail of toys behind them, we suggest this music system (although it may not *always* work!).

Role play and defunct ICT

One of the best and most cost-effective solutions to supporting children's independence in ICT is in the area of role play. As I said in the introduction to this chapter, children are surrounded by technology and they need to explore and make sense of it in meaningful contexts.

For example, when we go to the place that Daddy calls the 'hole-in-the-wall machine' he presses some buttons and money magically comes out.

For example, what happens when my big sister presses the buttons on her mobile phone?

If role-play areas are developed from observing children's interests, and by reflecting technology in everyday lives, the children can begin to play with pretend technology that will deepen their understanding. In this way children can gradually begin to make sense of the world about them.

There are many role-play technology toys on the market that range from simple to sophisticated. Some of the most effective, however, may be toys that children make for themselves. At the Centre all the children can independently access the Workshop, which has a range of collage materials, different-sized cardboard boxes and joining materials. Recently a child made a conveyor belt and scanner from tubes, paper and plastic lids, which was then taken into the role-play shop. He then spent a few days playing with his newly made toy, saying 'Beep!' every time a piece of plastic fruit was passed over the scanner part of his model. Giving him autonomy over his learning had enabled that child to deepen his knowledge and understanding of the world.

We also keep a huge box of defunct technology. Staff and parents collect old and useless pieces of equipment and children may find:

- keyboards
- computer mouse
- joysticks
- central heating programmers
- telephones
- mobiles
- flex
- foot pumps

- cassette recorders
- hairdryers
- vacuum cleaner hoses
- clocks
- and much more!

By allowing children to incorporate these pieces of technology into their imaginative play they are supported to make sense of their world. Given a small tool kit, some of these machines may be taken apart and the wondrous interiors of cogs, buttons and wheels are displayed.

Other children may want to join machines together to make a fabulous space rocket to take them to the moon! By giving children such open-ended resources and the freedom to play and explore at will, we can really extend their imaginative play. We have observed children who have additional needs, especially in the areas of communication and co-ordination, who have particularly enjoyed play with defunct technology.

With the sensitive support of an adult, play can be developed and new vocabulary introduced. Alongside this exploration we are always careful to talk about safety. Children are told that these are broken machines, and that they should never play with or take apart machines that are still working. Children should also never touch plugs or sockets – this is something only grown-ups should do. When three- and four-year-olds are given simple explanations and clear guidelines, they can generally be trusted to understand and follow these very well.

Encouraging independence at home

When showing parents around the nursery for the first time we have a fairly mixed response to the level of ICT on offer throughout the school. They range from parents who are totally enthusiastic and knowledgeable about ICT to those who think that children should not have access to technology at all.

In all of our communication with parents we emphasise the place of ICT in children's learning and how it will never replace the sensory experiences of sand, water and sticky clay. How we place huge importance on physical activity outside and why social and emotional development is so crucial at this stage. As we talk to families about the role of ICT in the nursery school, and as parents observe their children becoming independent and confident with technology, they begin to trust us and want to support their child in the best way that they can.

Here are a few suggestions on how we encourage this partnership.

- There is a computer in the entrance to the school where parents and children can play together. One dad recently remarked that he had no idea that his daughter could open programs by herself and operate the mouse so effectively.
- Parent helpers in the class are sometimes asked to play games with the children using various ICT resources. Some mums who were using remote control cars in the garden with the children began to plan fairly complex roadways and ramps as they saw the children progressing in their understanding.
- We lend very cheap tape recorders for parents and children to take home to listen to songs and rhymes related to current interests. This has been particularly effective

for families who have English as an additional language, as they can record songs from their own culture. The children in the class are then able to listen to these at circle time and some have learnt simple songs in different languages.

- Talking book albums or cards are another brilliant resource that can be shared at home. These are photo albums or cards with pockets to house photographs or even children's drawings. On each page there is a button that can be pressed to record a few sentences. Children have taken the book home and put in photos of home and recorded a few sentences with their family. When the child shows the adults how to operate the book at home, this is a boost to independent learning and high self-esteem.

- The digital camera has been an asset for showing parents how happy, independent and settled their child is in those first few days of starting nursery. Many practitioners are very familiar with the problems of separating tearful children from their adults. Sometimes mums will leave reluctantly, thinking their child is miserable all morning, when really they have cheered up as soon as they have shut the classroom door! We now take a photograph of the child happily and independently playing and then quickly take this out to show Mum before she leaves. Since doing this we have found that trust builds up much more quickly, and parents become more confident. This has a positive effect on their children, and settling time has very much improved. This has been particularly beneficial with children who have additional needs and who often are taxied into school – a photograph sent home can make all the difference.

Conclusion

I hope that I have persuaded you that by giving children control over technology, their understanding is deepened and they can begin to naturally incorporate elements of ICT in their play to support other areas of learning in a meaningful way.

Children who are growing up in a technological world show no fear of pressing buttons to see what happens. I think that we owe it to them as adults to encourage this confidence, allowing them to explore and experiment so that they will grow up without some of the hang-ups about ICT that many of us experience.

I hope also that I have shown you that independence in ICT is not just about expensive resources. Junk modelling, role play and defunct technology are all equally valid.

Why not choose just one small area in which you would like children to increase their independence and observe what happens?

3 ICT and children's creativity

Harriet Price

Introduction

Creative development is its own area of learning within the Early Years Foundation Stage (EYFS) and this is employed to capture children's development in:

- Responding to Experiences, Expressing and Communicating Ideas
- Exploring Media and Materials
- Creating Music and Dance
- Developing Imagination and Imaginative Play.

The National Curriculum Handbook (1999) included creativity within the section on thinking skills. It stated that: 'Creative thinking skills . . . enable pupils to generate and extend ideas, to suggest hypotheses, to apply imagination and to look for alternative innovative outcomes.'

The EYFS also has a commitment to:

- Creativity and Critical Thinking.

This is one of four commitments to the principle of Learning and Development that states: 'Children learn and develop in different ways and at different rates and all areas of Learning and Development are equally important and inter-connected.'

It is this inter-connectedness that will underlie the references to children's creativity within this chapter. As the EYFS conveys, creativity does not sit within any single project, or simply within the arts, but is a way of being, seeing and interacting with the world.

So what is creativity?

There has been a long history of recognising creativity in Early Years childhood education. It has been a major focus of work from many of the great early childhood theorists including Piaget, Montessori, Vygotsky and Bruner. It lies at the heart of the philosophy of Loris Malaguzzi and his work at Reggio Emilia. Creativity has been part of projects such as High Scope and is reflected in theories of cognitive development and intelligence, for example, Gardner's theory of multiple intelligences. It is beyond the scope of this book to discuss these great works here. I do not wish to simplify or ignore the enormous amount of insightful work that has been written on creativity in childhood, but to pay homage to that, and know that everything we draw on in our present-day good practice has arisen out of the benefit of such great theorists and practitioners.

For the purposes of this chapter we can use a pragmatic definition that helps us to identify closely what creativity is so that we can recognise it when we see it, nurture and encourage it, and celebrate achievements in creativity in learning and teaching. There is no definitive definition of creativity, and in our work with such young children we can adopt an inclusive approach where each child can be considered to have creative potential, and to be capable of creative expression.

Creativity is about discovering the new or making new connections. In this case, for very young children much of what they do, say and think as they play each day is unique and original to them and as such can be defined as creative. We can all think of examples of this. A child's spoken language offers particularly delightful and often humorous examples. A child travelling in a car asked when we were going to go across the 'La, la, las', and these turned out to be the speed bumps in the road as they jolted her into singing 'La, la, la'.

Perhaps a child knows best when they are being creative. This is the thinking of Loris Malaguzzi, who helped to establish Reggio Emilia, an approach to creativity and learning which takes its name from the northern Italian city in which he is based. He places a large emphasis on the views of children: 'They are the best evaluators and most sensitive judges of the values and usefulness of creativity' (Edwards *et al*. 1993).

Loris Malaguzzi created a forum where children are encouraged to depict their understanding through one of the '100 languages of children', which refers to their unlimited creative potential. He believes that when we perceive children as strong, capable and creative, we inspire them to the height of their creative potential. Instead of seeing children as empty vessels that need filling up with information and knowledge, he sees them as already full of creative potential and artists in their own right: 'Each child is unique and the protagonist of his or her own growth. Children desire to acquire knowledge, have much capacity for curiosity and amazement, and yearn to create relationships with others and communicate' (Edwards *et al*. 1993).

With keen observation and by coming to know children well, practitioners can begin to recognise a child's creative acts, whether these are in thought or spoken language, role play, mark making, physical movement, making and building, in creating sounds and music or in any of their '100 languages'. We can observe children's creative acts by noticing how meaningful they are to the child. We can view the level of engagement the child has with the process, the pleasure they take and their focus of attention and interest.

Loris Malaguzzi says: 'Creativity becomes more visible when adults try to be more attentive to the cognitive processes of children than to the results they achieve in various fields of doing and understanding' (Edwards *et al*. 1993). We are arriving at an understanding of creativity being part of children's unique interaction and ways of seeing and making sense of the world around them. We can see this creativity by observing and knowing children themselves and not by focusing on end products. Creativity is about process: in the early years of childhood it may result in an end product, but may well not. We need to engage in and capture the processes to support children's creativity. It follows then that we can support children's creativity through observing and evaluating their play, building carefully on what they are engaged with and interested in, and interacting sensitively in that play to enable a child's own unique expression.

The EYFS commitment to creativity and critical thinking gives guidance in supporting creativity through making connections and transforming understanding. Some of the points it makes are:

- Being creative involves the whole curriculum, not just the arts. It is not necessarily about making an end product such as a picture, song or play.
- Children will more easily make connections between things they've learnt if the environment encourages them to do so. For example, they need to be able to fetch materials easily and to move them from one place to another.
- New connections help to transform our understanding but this can often be a long process.

Children do not learn and develop in isolation; they learn alongside their peers and through interaction with adults. Loris Malaguzzi makes a number of observations about the optimum conditions for developing creativity in children's daily experience, including an emphasis on interaction with adults and peers: 'The most favourable situation for creativity seems to be interpersonal exchange, with negotiation of conflicts and comparison of ideas and actions being the decisive elements' (Edwards *et al.* 1993).

It is possible to stifle creativity and Early Years practitioners need to be careful not to over-structure children's learning or to provide insufficient time for sustained play, thus cutting off children's opportunities for developing creativity.

Practitioners must provide a balance for children between structure and freedom of expression that will make a space for their creativity to develop. We can encourage, nurture and extend children's creativity through our relationships and interactions with them.

We need to provide ICT in ways that support our pedagogy and our understanding about the nature of young children's developing creativity. This will best be achieved through providing children with a wide range of open-ended and meaningful ICT experiences with plenty of opportunities to explore and interact with others. We also need to model using ICT creatively to cultivate an environment where creativity can shine.

Practitioners using ICT creatively

One way practitioners can explore their own creativity, and model their creativity for children, is through using ICT to document children's learning.

Documenting children's learning in the form of observing and recording of their ongoing achievements is central to Early Years practice. It is the basis for planned work. The work at Reggio Emilia is internationally recognised and has taught us much about this key pedagogic tool, which focuses more intensively on children's experience, memories and thoughts, and aims to capture the processes of learning.

Through documenting and sharing children's learning with themselves, each other and their families, we can:

- make learning visible;
- engage children further in the learning process through reflecting on experiences, so clarifying and deepening their understanding;
- stimulate children through learning from each other;
- build on children's sense of identity and their relationships by revisiting experiences and taking pleasure in their learning;
- share our interest in children's learning, showing them that their intentions, ideas and views are important to us and their families;
- put children and their processes of learning at the centre of our understanding for planning for children's next steps;
- encourage the development of shared meanings and experiences between a group of children, their families and other adults and lead into further planning.

As Loris Malaguzzi says, through documentation children 'become even more curious, interested, and confident as they contemplate the meaning of what they have achieved' (Edwards *et al.* 1993).

Technology offers us new and powerful ways to document the learning process. To help us, there are:

- a full range of cameras, including webcams and wireless webcams, to capture digital still and moving images with all the advantages of immediacy that digital cameras provide;
- interactive whiteboards to quickly display children's experiences through digital images and audio recordings;
- audio recorders of all kinds, Dictaphones, MP3 players, PDAs, microphones attached to tape-recorders or computers. These do not necessarily need transcribing; they can be shared with parents, children and other professionals digitally;
- computer software, such as PowerPoint, to share the journey children take through their learning. PowerPoint can include photos, audio, examples of children's work done on a computer, and teacher and child written comments;
- projectors, screens, interactive whiteboards, plasma screens to share displays with large groups of children, parents and other adults;
- software programs to make books for children about their experiences;
- talking cards and photo albums to quickly capture children's comments on their learning and to share with their friends and families.

(See Appendix 1, Software and resources.)

To use these tools creatively and effectively, practitioners need to become very familiar with them, allowing themselves time to explore their possibilities and to become confident in their uses. The list above is long and could be daunting for those who do not consider themselves to be technically minded. If this is the case just start with one tool, investigate some of the ways you could use it to develop documenting children's learning and become confident in your practice. It is not a question of how much technology you use but of using the technology you choose skilfully and imaginatively.

For example, most practitioners are using digital cameras. If you are not already doing so, try developing the way you take photographs.

Let us take an example of children engaged in making a construction.

You might take photographs of the processes of children building the construction. Use the zoom on your camera to take some close action shots of the children's hands as they carefully balance the blocks, and to capture their expressions of concentration as they collaborate. Try to capture the whole process of construction as it develops. Print the photographs out and display them in a different way from usual, perhaps overlapping the photographs with the ultimate construction (or the demolition!) in the middle. Or create a slideshow of the photographs and add it to the screensaver on a computer for the children to come back to and discuss, or display it through a larger screen for families to engage in the processes of their children's learning.

This could be developed further with some knowledge of PowerPoint or children's software that allows them to create a story. Add the photographs with the children, once you feel competent, and record their comments and your reflections, either through a microphone or by written text. Or you could make a book of the children building the construction. This could be a printout from the PowerPoint or software used, or photographs could be added to a 'talking book' and children's comments recorded.

Figure 3.1

If you feel confident with all of the above, try taking some video clips as the children build and add these to the electronic version of their learning journey. If your video recorder has the facility for recording audio at the same time, then make sure you are reasonably close to the children when you record, or add an external microphone. Many digital still cameras record audio clips, and this is a really simple way of adding video, but not all record sound.

Take video of real-world building sites, run it on a computer as a background to children's play or to look at and talk about it together.

For those with interactive whiteboards you could add the photographs to the gallery and encourage children to make a display of what they were doing, through dragging and dropping the photographs onto the main screen. They could rearrange the photographs into the order of the construction being built or they might choose to put photographs that are most meaningful for them onto the main screen. Capture their reflections through written text on the board, or through the interactive whiteboard's 'Recorder', and share with each other and the children's families.

Building a construction out of blocks is a standard activity in most Early Years settings but we can see from the examples above how documenting this and sharing this learning with the children will take on whole new forms of learning.

At whatever stage you are with your own skills at using technology, you can be creative in its uses. Think of other technology around you and think about how you could be using it more creatively. The suggestions below for developing children's creative uses of technology might give you further ideas. Share your learning with children, enjoying and modelling your own creative processes.

Using ICT to support and develop young children's creativity

The following are ideas and projects you can adapt for your own context. They are not intended as a bank of activities but are there to draw on and adapt for particular children and particular moments according to your observations of children's play, interests, ability and knowledge. Remember; creativity is not inherent within these ideas or experiences, creativity comes from the child. These ideas have the potential to spark creativity, but bear in mind that children need:

- **Time** to be creative, to express themselves and to develop their creative skills
- **Freedom** to be creative when they want to be
- **Support** in developing their creativity and skills
- **Choices** of a range of creative media
- **Inspiration**, a starting point to get them going.

Digital cameras

See all of the ideas for using a digital camera in Appendix 2.

- Take photographs of the children's creative play and use them to exchange ideas and share meanings (see above on documenting children's learning).
- Support children in developing their own use of a digital camera and encourage them to reflect on the photographs they have taken, sharing the choices they have made.
- Use digital cameras to look more closely at natural objects and use the photographs as a stimulus for art and creative work.

Figure 3.2

Figure 3.3

Video cameras

Show children how to use a video camera, such as the movie maker camera (see Appendix 1 and Appendix 5). Give them plenty of opportunities to freely practise using it.

Young children will enjoy exploring their own playful uses of the camera and we need to give them time for this and not attempt to structure their uses too soon or too often. Once children have had plenty of opportunities to explore the camera, to practise and rehearse how it works and how to use it, then they will be ready for sharing a planned use of the camera.

Figure 3.4

- Observe children's playful uses and build on these. Outdoors I saw a child taking video of another child popping in and out of a box like a jack-in-the-box. She was directing the action and had a lovely fun idea for a short movie. We saw friends of hers coming out of the play house. I suggested she could do a similar thing with someone ringing the door bell and her friends popping out of the door in turn. She took ownership of this idea and her friends enjoyed acting their parts. After her directing and filming she put the movie together, with support, in the Movie Maker software. Sharing it with friends led to other children being stimulated to become 'directors', 'camera crew' or 'actors' themselves.
- Video children's play as characters from story books or acting out well-loved tales.

Scanners

- Scan in children's creations: paintings, drawings, collages and, along with photographs of the making processes, adding them to children's 'learning journeys' (see above on documenting children's learning).
- Scan pictures into PowerPoint to make animated stories. Record the children's combined stories using written text or audio.
- Use a scanner to import non-digital photographs, useful for when children bring in photos from home. Use as digital photographs; add to art, story making or presentation software, into a slide show, or into the 'gallery' part of interactive whiteboard software for children to add borders or arrange in a sequence.
- Scan in natural objects, and show children how they can rearrange them to get the effect they want. This can be extended to printing the pictures, laminating them and using them as table mats.

Webcams

Webcams can work as cheap digital cameras. Adding a USB extension lead means the webcam can be moved quite a distance from the computer. Webcams usually have a button on them for taking still images, or children can use the webcam software to take photos or video.

Using wireless webcams, try to do the following:

- Encourage children to record the process of an activity as they progress through it, documenting their own learning.
- Leave the webcam on and let children be stimulated by seeing themselves on camera. This can lead to many uses: singing, sharing a story and seeing themselves reading the story, recording still or moving images of work or dressing up for the camera.
- Record the children singing as a group.
- Work with a partner in the Early Years setting to share favourite rhymes and songs across the Internet.

Art software

Art programs allow children to do things they would not be able to do outside of the software. They often offer tools, such as a rainbow of colours in one stroke or creating shapes like stars. They provide 'clean' art; children can instantly and completely rub out, undo or start again, allowing endless opportunities for exploring and investigating. Children can mix media, combining digital and traditional media.

Art programs give children's mark making a certain kind of equality. They might be interpreted as limiting creativity but they can be particularly useful for children with individual needs or who lack confidence in their own mark making.

- Model uses of the software yourselves: make a repeat pattern and print out for wrapping paper (2Simple's 2Paint a Picture 'Pattern' tool makes this an easy process: see Appendix 1).
- Model the uses of the art program, teaching children how to use each of the tools according to their own levels of competence and interest.
- Stimulate children's interest by starting a blank 'page'. Paint and save an outline of a spaceship, shop or night sky. The children can then paint over the top of these, using tools and clip art to fill with objects or decorate with patterns, stars and fireworks.
- Take a photo with a digital camera, or copy a photo from Google Image search, open it in a paint program and paint over the top.
- Copy a photo from Google Image search, (for example, of an artist's work), open it in a paint program and crop half of the image away, leaving the blank half for children to fill in with the artist's work as the starting point.
- Clown faces – take a photo of a face and paint on top. Be sensitive about this and make sure children are happy to paint over their faces.
- Decorated elephants – find a plain photo of an elephant on the Internet, and decorate in the style of Indian elephants.

- Scan in a copy of a hand to paint on top for Mendhi patterns (use a natural paint program, such as Revelation Natural Art, which has simulated watercolours, to paint over the top of images. This will allow the image to show through still. See Appendix 1). Or scan in a Pixie cover and decorate to transform a Pixie into a character (See resources Appendix 1).
- Import a birthday photograph of a child and decorate it with birthday clip art.
- Print off a 'painting' and add it to the creative area for children to carry on with, using traditional media. Children can add to their painting or cut parts out and add them to their other creations.
- Scan traditional painted or drawn children's work into an art program and paint into it (combining media helps children to look at their art works in different ways and involves them in 'real-life' artists' uses of a computer, helping them adopt it as a tool for learning and not see it just as a 'games machine').

Programmable toys

- Tape white chalk to the back of Pixie and draw using Pixie on large sheets of black paper.
- Tape pens, or use a Pixie 'scribble pack' to draw with Pixie; children are fascinated by the round shapes this rectangular box can make.
- Print out Pixie covers for children to transform Pixie into a story book character. Use with a Pixie grid (make this by drawing out the columns and rows Pixie can travel along) with a few scanned and reduced images from the book to represent the places the character travels to in the story. For example, the Pixie could be Little Red Riding Hood and the board could include images of her house, a forest, flowers, her grandmother's cottage and the wolf dressed as the grandmother inside the cottage.

Smart boards

Smart boards are a type of interactive whiteboard (IWB). They are especially appropriate for very young children because they operate through finger touch. This makes drawing, rubbing out and moving objects on the board a very sensory experience. The large screen allows for greater collaboration than a computer screen, which means more opportunities for interacting with children over their ideas and sharing these as a group. Become very familiar with all the smart board tools by using the 'Help' button at the top of the smart notebook. There are endless ideas for using IWBs to support children's creativity (see the Resources area of Foundation.e2bn.org for further ideas). Here are just a few:

- An excellent use of smart boards is to use them in conjunction with good quality art software. As children make marks, show them what the range of tools can do. Model using the tools and then stand back and watch what the children do with them.

- Model using the board to make designs: make a design for a playdough model, a pattern for wrapping paper or to add to a model.
- Scaffold children's uses of the Gallery clip art to retell traditional tales or piece together a nursery rhyme.
- Add more clip art and photos of the children to the Gallery for children to retell events, such as going to the park, or to make up their own stories.
- Add peripherals, such as a visualiser or a digital microscope. Look at natural materials, print and add to art works.

Overhead projectors and light boxes

- Set up translucent objects next to a light box for children to add, rearrange and create new shapes.
- Set up collections next to an overhead projector pointing to a large screen (preferably in a dark space) for children to add, rearrange and create shapes. Natural objects work well, including leaves, twigs and feathers. The children will explore and may like to discover what happens when they stand in front of the projected image.
- Set up collections with an overhead projector pointing to a wall covered in white paper, or a flip chart. Encourage the children to explore the shapes these make through drawing on the paper.

Figure 3.5

Role-play toys

- Be creative in your provision of everyday technology. Add defunct mobile phones to pockets in children's dressing-up clothes, add a torch in the cupboard under the sink for the 'plumber', or in a 'garage' to look underneath a car, or add a 'baby monitor' to a doll area.

Figure 3.6

- Add a computer and role-play software to role play: for example, add 'At the Doctor's' to children's doctor or hospital play. This will help make the 'surgery' or 'hospital' more realistic and support children in meaningful play and in making connections.
- Make 'role-play boxes'. These are an easy way to manage supporting children's spontaneous play. Add ICT elements such as walkie-talkies, torches, mobile phones, defunct cameras, timers, key fobs, small metal detectors, calculators, drilling machines, voice changers, MP3 microphones and so on.
- Use a computer to print out prescriptions, or stock-taking charts for the children to fill in. Print out signs and notices with the children, for shops, surgeries, parks, buses and trains.

Figure 3.7

- Make some cardboard mock-up machines, or use defunct technology: cardboard petrol pumps, televisions, cash machines or old phones, tape recorders, microphones, headsets, mice and computer keyboards. See Chapter 5 for more about defunct technology.

Computers

Encourage children to see the computer as a tool for their learning. Use the computer for 'away from the computer' experiences. Create a balance between content-based software, such as Maths or Literacy software and content-free software, such as an art program or an Early Years word processor. The latter will allow for children's creativity and can link with children's experiences in and out of the setting.

- Demonstrate uses of the computer to make signs, lists, labels, envelopes, notices, etc. for role play.
- Develop children's creative thinking by following up their interests with them through Internet searches: for example, by finding images of car badges or watching elephants in the wild through a live webcam.
- Use peripherals, such as scanner, webcam, microphone, camera, microscope, to make the most of the computer's creative opportunities.
- Use all the ideas for scanners, webcams, digital and video cameras, smart boards and art software given above to develop children's creativity through a computer.
- With children, add speech bubbles to their photographs and support them in putting in what they want to say. With experience children can do this themselves with an Early Years desktop publishing program, allowing them greater opportunities for being creative with their photographs.
- Create cards for celebrations, send e-cards to each other through websites such as CBeebies or Spot the Dog.
- Add photos of the children at play to the screensaver.
- Model your own creative uses of a computer, and children will quickly join in!

Music, sound recorders and listening devices

Music and technology have been hand in glove for a very long time. Think back to the invention of the phonograph by Thomas Edison in 1877, the start of the electric guitar in American music in the 1930s, and the advent of the synthesiser in the 1960s by Robert Moog. Musicians have always been willing to embrace technology to make their compositions permanent, for an individual to sound like an ensemble, and to develop new techniques and sounds.

Music technology is all around us and in daily use: (radios, cassette and CD players), and the new technologies: (DAB radio and MP3 and MP4 players). I have added sound recorders and listening devices to this section, although they can equally be used for speaking and listening, not just for music.

- Children love to play at being 'pop stars'. Give their role play a musical theme: a musical instrument shop or a 'record' shop. Alternatively, it could be a recording

studio where a band can practise and record their music. Provide play guitars, voice changers, karaoke machines and MP3 microphones and headsets.
• Electronic keyboards are wonderful for investigating and exploring sounds.
• Provide a recording device such as a tape recorder, Dictaphone or MP3 microphone, for the children to record their compositions.
• Use the sounds on a Mixman 2 to explore music from different cultures: Indian, reggae, Latin and more. Mixman 2 connects to your computer and turns it into a DJ mixing desk.

Figure 3.8

Figure 3.9

- Use Early Years Music software such as 2Simple's 2Play from their music toolkit to compose sounds and music. Talk to the children about the feeling of the music. This is well illustrated in the software program Musical Leaps and Bounds, where a blank television set plays particularly sad, happy or dreamy sounding music and a button press shows images of a dog expressing the mood of the music. Encourage the children to think about the feeling they want to express in their music making.
- Use their compositions as backgrounds to stories the children create with you, or as a background to their photographs, in PowerPoint or story-creating software.
- Musical Leaps and Bounds can stimulate dance. The screens are introduced through dancing characters that children (and adults!) love to imitate. This can be taken further in a screen that allows you to sequence dance moves. Children can have a go at planning a sequence of moves for an onscreen character that they can then copy. Beware: help children keep to simple and repetitious moves; it goes very fast!

Summary

All of the above is a daunting list for leaders and practitioners, if it was thought we needed to provide all of these resources and such a vast range of experiences (some needing high levels of technical expertise on our part) to support children's creativity. But appropriate uses of technology are about quality of provision, management, careful observation and matching with child development, interests and skilful adult interactions. Select a few chosen resources that you can manage. Get to know them well and then develop their uses alongside children's play. Be creative in your uses and watch how the children adopt them in their play. As Loris Malaguzzi said: 'Stand aside for a while and leave room for learning, observe carefully what children do and then, if you have understood well, perhaps teaching will be different from before.'

4 Giving children a voice by using ICT

Karen James and Chris Cane

Introduction

Working in Early Years settings supporting children from birth to five, the Brent Early Years and ICT teams have seen how ICT can contribute powerfully to young children's learning. In this chapter we provide examples and case studies of the many ways that ICT equipment can give young children a voice. It includes findings from pilot schemes, training sessions and projects showing different ways that ICT equipment has been used and the impact on individual children.

Approach to ICT

After visiting Gamesley Early Excellence Centre in Glossop we felt that we wanted to adopt their approach to ICT, by using a wide range of battery-operated and electrical items. We were very keen to ensure that ICT should be seen as a tool to enhance learning in all areas of the curriculum and so ICT became one of our priorities in the Early Years.

Giving children a voice

Following from our strong tradition of consulting children in Brent, we recognised that it is more difficult to involve very young children in this process. The UN Convention on the Rights of the Child Article 12, adopted by the UK in 1991, gives children the right to say what they think should happen when adults are making decisions that affect them, and to have their opinions taken into account. However, we were concerned that many young children found it difficult to express their ideas in ways that adults in their settings could easily understand. In Brent we have been involved in the Listening to Young Children project developed by the Coram Family Trust (Lancaster 2003) and were committed to finding ways to give young children a voice. We felt that using non-computer-based ICT equipment would not only provide a 'way in' but would also be important in 'creating a context in which voices are encouraged' (2003: 5). This would empower young children and enable their voices to be heard.

The views of boys, of children with English as an Additional Language (EAL) and of some cultural and ethnic groups may also be difficult to access. We were particularly concerned about Black African and Caribbean boys we have identified as a vulnerable group at risk of under-achievement. We wanted to provide meaningful learning experiences for young boys in these groups to promote high levels of engagement.

Children's perspective

ICT was highly effective in helping to capture how children and families had been consulted. It also provided the medium through which children could comment on their learning. With the new Ofsted framework (2005) looking at the setting through the eyes of the children, we used videos and photos to provide a lens to see things from the child's perspective. On several occasions practitioners were stunned by the quality of the children's photos. Becoming more familiar with their own appearance and their role within the setting was a key factor in enabling the children to express themselves.

Outline of project

Brent has run several Early Years projects involving ICT:

- loan scheme of non-computer-based resources
- outdoor project
- Listening to Young Children
- DfES funded project using ICT in the Foundation Stage.

Loan scheme

We drew up a list of recommended ICT resources for settings and schools and compiled some resource boxes, which were available for loan. Settings and schools that borrowed the boxes were asked to evaluate the resources and document their findings. Each box had a particular focus: for example, role play, light and discovery or music and dance. Practitioners began to notice the interesting and creative ways in which the children were using the resources. Feedback indicated that the children responded in ways that the practitioners did not expect. The resources seemed to have a significant impact on children with special needs, giving them a previously untapped means of expression.

Outdoor project

Over a number of years Brent has promoted learning outdoors in all its Early Years settings. We began to develop ways to use ICT outdoors, particularly to promote role play (Bilton *et al.* 2005: 92). By looking at how children use the outdoor area and by building on their interests we realised that they used ICT equipment outdoors very confidently. Some children began to talk for the first time in the setting when using ICT equipment outdoors. In the outdoor environment children seemed less inhibited and were able to make more noise. When combined with ICT this enabled children to express themselves more freely.

Listening to Young Children

In our work with a number of settings developing the approach suggested by the Coram Family Trust, we asked children to record what they do or do not like about their setting by taking digital photographs. This convinced us that three- to five-year-olds were able to use digital video cameras effectively. It also showed us that digital images are a powerful way of enabling children's views to be heard. Children who may not be able to express themselves verbally can do so by taking photographs to represent their views.

This also helped practitioners to understand how children viewed the setting and which areas were important to them, notably cloakrooms and the outdoor area.

The children enjoyed using the video as a magnifying glass to look very closely at their friends' faces, into brickwork and other crevices. Some even made video clips of themselves by reversing the view finder.

Shohaib

A practitioner observed, 'Shohaib spent 10–15 minutes taking a movie outside. He began to talk to other children when filming them (not children he would normally interact with). He came to me at one point and said, "It's only me, it's only me!" He had turned the screen around so I explained how to turn it back.

'Later on I saw him lying in a tyre, filming himself. As he videoed himself Shohaib appeared to be luxuriating in his own image, taking a long time to make it really special. He used the video camera like a magnifying glass, revelling in looking at his face and the different emotions he can express. Many young children enjoy seeing themselves on film and talking about what they are doing.'

Foundation Stage ICT project

Funding from the DfES enabled us to run a Foundation Stage project using ICT. Our project focused on using non-computer-based ICT equipment outdoors to promote speaking and listening skills. The target group of Black African and Caribbean boys had a range of difficulties with speaking and listening, social skills or lack of engagement. Based on evidence from previous projects we selected resources (see Table 4.1), which we felt would be particularly effective. Both ICT resources and learning outdoors are known to promote confidence with communication (Bilton *et al.* 2005, Siraj-Blatchford and Siraj-Blatchford 2003). However we did not realise that for many children using ICT equipment outdoors, including video cameras, voice recorders and voice changers, would prove to be transformational. Practitioners were making comments such as 'The children are blossoming' and 'He's a different child'.

An important part of the project was to look at the role of ICT in documenting children's learning following the Reggio Emilia approach (Edwards *et al.* 1993). This involved both children and practitioners using video cameras to record, reflect on and document learning.

The project had a clear structure of training, network meetings, visits from advisory staff and support from headteachers. We set up regular network meetings to develop collaboration, with an ethos of learning together. These meetings became a crucial support system for the project practitioners, enabling them to share good practice and to develop their own ICT competence.

Using ICT equipment outdoors

Very quickly children became skilled in using the non-computer-based ICT equipment and practitioners were happy to let children use video cameras outdoors. Soon we were hearing of the dramatic effects on children in each of the settings. ICT equipment held particular appeal for young boys and they began to talk more while on the move. This had a positive effect on practitioners' motivation because they could see the impact their input had on children's learning.

The children were trusted to use expensive equipment like video cameras and voice recorders outdoors after developing safety rules together. Laces were attached to pieces of equipment so they could hang safely round the children's necks, allowing them to run off suddenly with no danger of the equipment being lost or damaged. The children took responsibility for equipment, reminding each other how to use it safely. All the video cameras lasted without any breakages throughout the project, summarised by Shane's comment, 'It's great using these – you got to be sensible.'

Resources

The items in Table 4.1 enabled children to talk to each other and develop their confidence to express their ideas and opinions. Some pieces of equipment gave young children a voice in ways that we had not anticipated.

Examples of how some pieces of equipment were used

Remote control car: Nathan

While experimenting with a remote control car, some children who were very quiet or unable to express their ideas easily showed improvements in the length and complexity of sentences that they used. They moved from single word utterances, usually heard inside school, to longer utterances: for example, predictions about how the remote control car would move on different surfaces.

'WOW! I was amazed at his concentration. A light bulb went on in his head when he tried the car on different surfaces.'

Table 4.1

ICT equipment	Linked case study
Video camera	Nicholas
Karaoke machine	Abukhar, Amir
Voice changer	Jamaican child
Voice recorder	Marosh, Yusef
Walkie-talkies	Pam and the ants
Channel headset	Shane
Remote control car	Nathan
Headlamp torch	
Cassette recorder	
Talking photo album	
Sound button	
Metal detector	

Channel headset: Shane

While playing with the channel headsets, Shane exhibited a relaxed and confident manner, which the practitioner had not seen in previous paired activities. Shane and his friend ran around the playground talking to each other on the headsets, playing hide and seek. When they talked about their learning afterwards the children were very excited and their language skills improved.

Figure 4.1

N: I liked talking to each other.
S: It's good when you are further away and hiding.
N: It feels nice and comfy.

Outcomes

Using ICT equipment gave the children a voice in a number of different ways. However, it is the way that practitioners approached the project and the trust that they placed in the children that underpinned all the outcomes we observed. Below are some of the most memorable, illustrated by individual case studies.

Child who had not spoken in the setting literally given a voice

Marosh

Marosh arrived from India at the beginning of the school year. While at school she did not feel comfortable communicating verbally in either English or her home language. Sending the voice recorder home with Marosh enabled the staff to hear her voice for the first time, so ICT literally gave her a voice. The school and the family both gained an insight into what she knew and was learning. Her father was able to share her learning with the practitioners, delighting in her achievements. For example, he sent back voice samples of songs that Marosh had learnt at school. The practitioners were reassured that Marosh spoke English at home and recalled many of the activities that she encountered in the Reception class. Both the voice recorder and the voice changer seemed to act as a prop for her. At the end of the project Marosh still did not speak distinctly, but she giggled and communicated with other children and spoke in a soft whispery voice into the voice changer.

Children with SEN able to express themselves

Amir

A three-year-old boy at a local day care setting was reluctant to talk after a recent traumatic experience. He had not been heard to talk in the setting for several months, even to his peers. One day the practitioners introduced a karaoke machine to the group. Later that week they heard a voice singing loudly. The manager hurried in, ready to say, 'Be quiet', but she soon changed her mind when she saw who was speaking. Amir then went on to tell a story to the whole group while holding the microphone. The practitioners watched in amazement.

Nicholas

Nicholas had only a few friends and spoke briefly to adults and children. He was inclined to be on the edges of class activities and often appeared disengaged. It came as a great surprise to his teacher when Nicholas picked up the video camera and began using it confidently. He became an expert in video filming, which improved his status with his peers. He made a connection with his home experiences, saying that he had 'millions of video cameras at home'. The video camera also provided a stimulus for Nicholas to interact with other children. He became an interviewer and approached groups of children that he would not normally. He used the video to ask penetrating questions. Not satisfied with simple answers, he probed, asking, 'Yes, but what are you doing?', requiring more detail and urging them to 'Talk up, please.' Nicholas became more proactive in the classroom and his teacher capitalised on his unexpected affinity with ICT. He was able to help the adults download video clips to watch on the interactive whiteboard. These experiences led to Nicholas' self-image improving considerably.

Child becoming less self-conscious

A child who had recently arrived in England from Jamaica felt self-conscious about his accent. He was reluctant to communicate freely. He began to use the voice changers, which disguised his voice as a robot, spaceman and alien to communicate with other children. Soon he established new friendships and no longer needed to use ICT as a prop to hide behind, though ICT equipment had initially acted as an icebreaker and provided a different way of talking.

Figure 4.2

Children with EAL began to talk more confidently

Pam and the ants

Two nursery children with EAL used walkie-talkies throughout an afternoon to track, talk about and monitor an ant's movements. Both children usually spoke very little in the setting and rarely communicated with each other, so it was very surprising for Pam, the practitioner, to see them so involved in a sustained conversation together. The walkie-talkies provided the prop that maintained the children's interest and focus for their discussion.

Quiet child began to talk freely

Abukhar

'Abukhar is speaking out loud and answering questions with ease. We never really heard his voice before this project began. He really has used ICT as a prop to let his voice out.'

Figure 4.3

Sue's report

At the beginning of the project Abukhar only spoke very quietly and only really to meet his own needs. Even then we had to almost put our ear to his mouth to hear anything at all. When we first introduced the karaoke machine he really wanted a go, but when it was his turn he was unable to allow himself to speak. Tyriesse from Reception noticed this and came over and sat next to him. Tyriesse sang a song while staying very close to Abukhar. Abukhar began to laugh in a very open way. We had never seen him being so unguarded before. Then Tyriesse gave Abukhar the mic, while staying close to him, and Abukhar sang the whole song, 'Bob the Builder'. Later the same morning Abukhar was able to sing in a group. He now talks with ease to adults and children. Being able to speak comfortably is accelerating his progress in a way that would have been impossible before.

Figure 4.4

Children sharing their learning with their parents

Documentation: following the learning journey

Abukhar's rapid progress was recorded in photos and video clips by the astounded practitioners. Abukhar dragged his dad in to see these photos of his experiences with the karaoke machine, which were clearly displayed near the entrance. Abukhar's father, who rarely interacted with nursery staff, became involved in his son's learning, which later led to discussions with the practitioners. Having something to talk about for this Somalian father, who has English as an additional language, clearly helped him. It was especially inviting to have a visual prompt in a place that was highly visible and accessible to parents. For both Abukhar and his father it was the beginning of a new way of communicating within the school setting.

Learning with peers

Jabril

At the beginning of the project Jabril needed support in his interactions with adults and children. He needed encouragement to join in with class routines and preferred to socialise with boys. Using the video camera provided a way for Jabril to explore areas of the setting that he did not usually find attractive. Jabril was given responsibility for the video camera and was asked to video in the hairdresser role-play area. This may have inspired him to play there himself, though he would usually have been reluctant to engage in a 'girl-based activity'. It gave him the confidence to become a receptionist in the hairdresser's and even to resist the jeering of his peers. Seeing this, the practitioner consulted Jabril and his friends and included the children's interests and ideas in planning the curriculum. Together they created a barber's shop, where Jabril was able to express himself verbally rather than through inappropriate behaviour.

Jevonte

Jevonte began making a pirate costume and drew a pirate ship on a piece of paper and other pirate paraphernalia. Then Jevonte tried to film himself playing pirates with his friend. However, Jevonte found playing with the sword and using the video camera too difficult and asked his teacher to do it. When they watched it back on the video screen, Jevonte said to Leon, 'Do you remember what I said? I said you cut my belly but I didn't die. Do you remember that? Look I cut you with my sword.' Jevonte and Leon immediately returned to their play. Later they showed the group this video clip on the interactive whiteboard. The following day more children came to the creative area to make a pirate costume and play pirates too. Jevonte's interest in pirates has inspired other children in the class to join in.

Children teaching adults

Yusef

At the start of the project Yusef found it difficult to follow class rules. He also found it difficult to share equipment and adult attention. During the project Yusef developed a role for himself as the chair of various playground conversations. He was particularly interested in using the voice recorder both to dictate his own ideas and to record others' conversations. He carried the voice recorder around the playground with him and recorded endless conversations and monologues. As Yusef played them back he became more aware of the structure of conversation. Yusef developed a self-regulatory voice, which had a major impact on his learning. His teacher valued his knowledge of using ICT, and like many others he explained, explored and experimented without any of the anxieties held by the practitioners. Yusef became the expert in using the voice recorders and was happy to explain to other children how to use the controls. This improved Yusef's ability to share and take turns and extended his language and vocabulary.

Children contributing to planning

View of setting

Practitioners acquired a deeper understanding of what the children enjoyed and valued in the setting. Children had a different perspective, looking closely at toilets, low-level displays and the outdoor area, particularly the 'sky as a roof above them'. The practitioners were amazed at the quality of the footage. For many children this was the first time they had expressed an opinion about the provision and the opportunities available to them. The practitioners felt that it was extremely important to give weight to all children's ideas, including the target children, many of whom were quiet or on the fringes. They did not belong to the more vocal group who contributed regularly at group times or in one-to-one conversations with practitioners. For the first time this group had a valid way to express their ideas. They felt confident that their opinions were going to be included in curriculum planning. Being in control of a video camera helped them to express and assert themselves.

Benefits of the video camera in giving children a voice

The children recorded their learning using video cameras, voice recorders, talking photo albums and sound buttons. This equipment also helped children to 'relaunch' their experiences, which enabled information to be shared between child, parent and practitioners in a highly accessible way.

Figure 4.5

A video camera:

- acts as a prop allowing child to approach other children outside their social group;
- captures learning moments and allows children to revisit their experiences;
- when readily available, allows children to record what is important to them when they see it.

This may be because:

- children see the video camera being used as a meaningful way of recording events at home so they value it as a way to record their own communication;
- there is the appeal of 'real' equipment, especially for boys;
- it encourages collaborative working so children need to communicate with each other;
- videos are very motivating for many different children.

Relaunch of learning: children's understanding

Whether the setting had an interactive whiteboard, PC, laptop or used the video camera itself to replay the children's video clips, this proved a very effective means of helping children to 'relaunch' their learning experiences (Edwards *et al.* 1993). Looking at photos and video clips helped children to verbalise their learning by making it more accessible. The children seemed to feel comfortable when the videos were replayed and they prompted further thinking. Video recording appeared to act as a catalyst for children to begin to experiment and explore ways that their needs could be accommodated within the setting. It gave them confidence that their ideas would be viewed sympathetically and included in future plans.

For children with EAL the visual images supported their descriptions of their learning. Because they had made the videos themselves, children felt confident to describe what was happening. Using the interactive whiteboard, a number of children surprised practitioners by talking confidently to a group about their learning in a way that they would not have done previously. When a video clip is shared in a group it seems to deepen the learning and enable a wider community understanding.

Table 4.2

Equipment	Way it supported relaunch of experience
Digital voice recorder	Playing back transcripts of family dialogue recorded at home
Sound button	Playing back simple instructions
Talking photo album	Looking through photo albums and replaying messages linked to photos
Digital video recorder	Replaying video clips of children's play

A group of children who had been on a walk to the supermarket recreated their experience through small-world play. Issa and Mohammed acted out their story using play people, while Tyriesse used the video camera to film them. Together they replayed the video footage watching through the view finder. This took their play on to the next level, as they drew in extra houses and traffic lights. This cycle continued and considerably lengthened the time the boys spent playing.

ICT moving learning forward

Shadows

During a discussion about shadows children's responses to questions such as 'Can you lose your shadow?' and 'How do you make a shadow?' were video-recorded. Jonathan did not know whether his shadow would stick to him, so the practitioner took the group outside to investigate. This investigation was also recorded and later that day the clips were replayed to see what they had discovered. Jonathan's teacher asked if he knew now whether his shadow stuck to his feet. As he watched the video clip Jonathan could clearly see that when Ahmed jumped the shadow remained on the ground while Ahmed was in the air. His teacher talked about how he had learnt something new and showed him the first video when he did not know the answer. They then played the new clip where he did know. Jonathan said, 'That's so amazing.' Watching the videos made the children aware of how their learning progressed and they were able to reflect on this process. They were also able to articulate how they felt about their learning, both individually and as a community of learners.

Summary of findings

Importance of ICT in children's lives

ICT is a powerful tool in facilitating children's voice. Photographs and videos particularly appeal to young children and help them to discover who they really are. They also act as a catalyst for children's talk. 'That's me!' 'That's my mum.' 'That's Sue and that's me.' 'I got the camera', said Shohaib.

Target children became the 'experts' in using the equipment and showed other children how they worked. These high-status symbols were instantly desirable, representing 'real things' that their families were involved in using at home. Children have a very clear idea of which photos they have taken and can describe in detail what they have recorded. Items such as the karaoke machine, voice changers and walkie-talkies acted as props, which allowed children who were reluctant to talk to find their voice.

Figure 4.6

Benefits of using ICT outdoors to give children a voice

- Children had more freedom to express themselves outdoors.
- Children could talk while moving rapidly.
- Both the quantity and the quality of oral communication increased.
- The combination of a larger space and using ICT props encouraged communication within wider social groupings.
- Children could be louder yet not overwhelm each other, especially when using karaoke and voice changers.
- Children showed high levels of engagement and deep concentration.
- Children engaged in meaningful first-hand experiences which they were eager to talk about.

Parents were able to share in their children's learning

Practitioners began documenting in the Reggio Emilia style, using examples of the children's own photos and samples of work. Documentation walls showing children's learning journeys appeared. These provided an invitation for families to go into school and reduced their anxiety, particularly for parents with EAL. They were really interested in their children's learning.

Practitioners consulted with children and parents about the next steps in learning. The practitioners completely revised their approach to planning and could see the benefit of the Reggio Emilia approach.

'Once you've started working in this way there's no going back.'

> Pairs of children were taken on walks to their own houses and the journey was video-recorded. The children's comments on the way showed how confident they were as they described local features and made predictions about what they would see next. Children explained their learning excitedly to their family, who could then act as advocates for their children. Based on the photos and videos, Khy's mum talked about his learning and offered suggestions about taking it forward.

Involving children in planning their learning

Using ICT can blur the boundaries between the role of the adult and the child, but in order to give children a voice practitioners must be prepared to listen. The nature of the ICT equipment ensured that practitioners did listen. They were surprised that what the children had to say was so powerful.

Videos usually show the adult perspective, but because these children had recorded their own learning it made the practitioners aware of what the children were interested in. Learning was filtered through the children's eyes. It provided another way of looking and jarred the practitioners into thinking more deeply about what is important to children and how the setting can support them. Practitioners became more skilful in 'tuning into children' and they responded sensitively.

Practitioners provided opportunities for children to extend learning, not only taking photos but also talking about the learning process. It can be very difficult to access thoughts of young and very quiet children, especially those with EAL. ICT equipment acted as a bridge, especially for some children on the SEN register with behavioural difficulties.

Many adults find it difficult to interpret non-verbal communication, but using video cameras facilitated interpretation of children's movements, for example in breakdance and raps. It highlighted the importance of non-verbal communication as being equally powerful, as noted in the Foundation Stage Curriculum Guidance (2000). They gained insights into children's needs, especially those who less readily engage within the school setting/environment. When the children's videos were replayed it gave practitioners a second chance to make observations of the children's learning and gave them time to look again at the play and reflect on what the children were doing. This deeper understanding helped practitioners to value the children's contributions and to pose questions to develop their learning further.

Influencing the curriculum

Using ICT equipment gave the children confidence. It allowed them to have more freedom in their learning. Practitioners reviewed their approach thoughtfully and were happier to let the learning be child led. A more equal balance of what adults understand and what children need in order to get a broad and balanced curriculum emerged. As a result of this 'planning rethink' the foremost purpose became to meet the children's needs and interests rather than being purely curriculum driven.

Practitioners developed methods for planning the curriculum that included consulting with children, parents and staff.

Conclusion

For us it was a revelation to find that ICT was able to unlock children in a way that other strategies had not been able to. The target boys in particular benefited from the experiences that they were offered and felt that their ideas and concerns were valued. They were able to trust the staff involved, who in turn had placed so much trust in the children. The practitioners' new learning mirrored the children's learning. ICT empowered not only the children but also the staff.

As a local authority, bearing in mind that such young children can have a voice and can express themselves so clearly through ICT, we began to wonder what impact it could have on older children. The exercise also made us rethink our expectations about young children's learning and what they say about their learning. What was happening in the Foundation Stage was leading the way in how children were able to talk about and contribute to their learning. Using ICT equipment outdoors really had provided children with another way of talking.

5 ICT and the outdoor learning environment

Harriet Price

Introduction

At first glance ICT and the outdoors do not appear to go well together. Technological tools are generally not suited to the outdoors: often needing a power source, failing in the damp and dying in the rain, rarely robust enough to withstand the more open environment of outdoors. Why, then, incorporate technology into outdoor learning when it does not seem to be suited to the outdoors?

There are two overriding reasons that I would argue compel us to incorporate technology into outdoor play. The outdoors is where some children learn best and technology can offer motivating, captivating and new ways into that learning.

Why the outdoors at all?

The Early Years Foundation Stage (EYFS) tells us that:

- Being outdoors has a positive impact on children's sense of well-being and helps all aspects of children's development.
- Being outdoors offers opportunities for doing things in different ways and on a different scale than when indoors.
- It gives children first-hand contact with weather, seasons and the natural world.
- Outdoor environments offer children freedom to explore, use their senses, and be physically active and exuberant.

Learning through Landscapes' vision states:

- All children have the right to experience and enjoy the essential and special nature of being outdoors.
- Young children thrive and their minds and bodies develop best when they have free access to stimulating outdoor environments for learning through play and real experiences.
- Knowledgeable and enthusiastic adults are crucial to unlocking the potential of outdoors.

Learning through Landscapes underpin their vision with values and I have picked out a few of these here but it is well worth reading their document, which provides a rationale for the provision of outdoor play. It can be seen on the EYFS pages and a web address is given in Appendix 1.

Learning through Landscapes lists some core values:

*   Play is the most important activity for young children outside.
*   Outdoor provision can, and must, offer young children experiences which have a lot of meaning to them and are led by the child.
*   The outdoor space and curriculum must harness the special nature of the outdoors, to offer children what the indoors cannot. This should be the focus for outdoor provision, complementing and extending provision indoors.
*   Outdoors should be a dynamic, flexible and versatile place where children can choose, create, change and be in charge of their play environment.
*   Young children must have a rich outdoor environment full of irresistible stimuli, contexts for play, exploration and talk, plenty of real experiences and contact with the natural world and with the community.

In Issue 8 of *Children in Europe*, Matti Bergstrom, Emeritus Professor of Neurophysiology at the University of Helsinki, states that until the age of six or seven, the area of the brain that processes logic and order has not fully developed and children depend more on their inner feelings and what is important for them. Children must have access to space and freedom in order to **play** out their fantasies, which are vital in helping them to develop ideas, values and understand the world around them. They are the food for brain development and the raw material for creativity (see www.childreninscotland.org.uk/cie).

So these are some of the vital reasons, visions and values for providing children with quality outdoor play provision, and technology can fit in with this and add to the imaginative and creative outdoor learning environment that will encourage children's full potential.

These values can guide us in making the most appropriate provision to encourage, sustain and develop children's play and learning outdoors. Technology needs to fit in with these values and must not clash with them: the values underpin the essential nature of the outdoor learning environment for young children. It is important that we hold on to the reasons why we value outdoor play for young children and not be led by technology into inappropriate provision. We are providing technology outdoors because it can support, motivate, enhance and even lead into new forms of learning, and any ICT provision needs to be questioned in this light.

The outdoor environment is not just another classroom; it is a different kind of space. Outdoors is on a larger scale than indoors, vertically at least! We feel ourselves in a different kind of space, children can be noisier and messier and there is more scope for physical and sensory experiences. Things are less predictable outside: wind blows and alters structures that children are building; leaves and twigs interact with children's chosen play materials; there are stones and pebbles, dirt, grass, trees, mini-beasts, flowers, seeds, rain, puddles, sunshine, shadows, places to hide things in and places to discover. The outdoors is not as structured as the indoors and this is exactly what lends itself to children's imaginations. Ask any adult to recall an experience of playing as a child and invariably they will recall an event that happened outdoors.

Outdoors can provide different learning opportunities

- *For developing PSED skills*
  Being outside might help some children develop positive relationships with others. Sharing, turn taking, problem solving, negotiating might be easier for some children away from adults and with a greater sense of freedom of movement and use of space. The outdoors possibly allows more room for children to express their own choices and preferences, and with sensitive adult support this can lead to personal and emotional growth.

- *For developing a healthy attitude to the outdoors and increasing awareness of the natural world*
  Children are less able to play outdoors in our lives today. The growth in road traffic and shifts in the make-up and daily rhythms of families and communities have left children with fewer outdoor places to go. An Early Years setting may be one of the few places children coming there may be able to enjoy and become confident in the outdoors. Becoming increasingly aware of and taking pleasure in the natural world is a way into developing a sense of responsibility and care for the environment.

- *For developing self-confidence*
  Outdoors might feel like a more shared space for children, close to their personal experiences of gardens, outside homes, parks and rural spaces. When children are outdoors in a setting they may feel it is less 'owned' by the setting and by adults. This might help some children to bring more of themselves to their play, developing their confidence as they explore what they can do and enjoy just being.

- *For developing physical strength and co-ordination and enabling risk-taking*
  Greater space can lead to climbing, jumping, skipping, running, rolling, using louder voices and the joy and sheer exuberance of greater freedom of expression. Outdoor challenges can help children take risks and set their own parameters.

- *For encouraging independence, responsibility and autonomous learning*
  There are many meaningful opportunities for children to develop their personal independence outdoors: for example, as they take on and off outdoor clothes or make decisions about when they need to go indoors. Outside, children can move further away from adults. They are more likely to rely on themselves in spontaneous play and in interacting with others. They can be given greater freedom in selecting resources and making their own choices and decisions. It might be possible to combine resources more easily outside: for example, collecting water to add to sand or filling prams with leaves, and in this way being able to follow their own thoughts and intentions through and to trust themselves as learners.

- *For development of creativity*
  Children can have different opportunities to develop their creativity and individuality outside. Outdoor spaces can be messier and noisier, allowing children to explore materials more freely. Natural objects are more easily used, they can lead to different types of mark-making, such as transient art that doesn't require glue or tape and where the pleasure is wholly in the process. There is usually more space to spread out larger and co-operative pieces of work. Music can be made with objects around them and can be louder and link more freely to expressive movement. Children can be encouraged to observe the natural world and gain a sense of wonder and delight at the patterns, colours, shapes and life around them.

- *For the sensory and tactile experiences*
  Being outside gives children increased opportunities to explore spontaneously through their senses. The natural shapes, textures, colours and smells of leaves, gravel, dense or sandy earth, twigs, air and weather are just part of the environment outdoors and part of children's play.

Technology and the outdoor learning environment

It might seem surprising that, in a book on using technology with young children, quite so much has been written about the nature of the outdoor learning environment. After all, I am not an expert in this area and there are plenty of wonderful books written about outdoor learning that far supersede the points made here. This has been done because to make ICT truly effective and integrate it fully into young children's learning it cannot be a bolt-on and it most certainly must not undermine the hugely beneficial learning that playing outdoors can provide. In planning for using technology outdoors with young children we must learn and know the very particular benefits of outdoor learning and then underpin these with technology where it is appropriate. We need to plan first from the environment children are learning within and then how we can enhance this or add to the learning through using a range of technologies.

In using technology outdoors we want it to be compatible with:

- the use of space so there is room for freedom of movement and children can be physically active;
- the use of time so that children's spontaneous play and opportunities for collaboration and creativity are not interrupted with too many adult intentions or too structured experiences;
- the use of quiet so that there are spaces where children can just be, talk to a friend or reflect;
- opportunities that the space provides for playing with friends, imagining, creating and problem solving;
- opportunities to use materials and resources in different ways;
- challenges for children in developing their independence and autonomous learning.

We want to use ICT in ways that are compatible with all of the above as well as doing more. ICT can be an extremely motivating factor in learning for some children. It can be the tool children are willing to share and engage over, it can promote problem-solving and it can add to learning in ways that were not previously possible. For example, just think of all the ways we can develop learning now with the immediacy of still and moving digital images.

Managing technology outdoors

A contributing factor to planning for using technology outdoors is that, because of its more vulnerable nature in an all-weather space, it needs careful management. Children need to be shown exactly where to find a piece of equipment or a technology toy (this will often be indoors) and they need to know exactly where to return it to. They need masses of modelling by adults of collecting a piece of equipment, or encouraging a child to do so, and pointedly returning it to its rightful spot, or encouraging a child to do so. This is true of equipment indoors, of course, but whereas it will not matter if a digital camera is left on a shelf in an indoor role-play area, it will very obviously matter if this tool is left outside. Children also need reminding in their play about the technology that is available to them and what might be a useful tool to add to their play. In order to manage this, try to bear in mind that using ICT outdoors with young children is not about **quantity**, it is not about flooding a space with technology. It is also, as we have seen, not just about repeating the inside provision outdoors. It is about observing children's play, selecting carefully and planning for **quality** experiences.

The adult role

As we saw previously, Learning through Landscapes' vision states that:

- knowledgeable and enthusiastic adults are crucial to unlocking the potential of outdoors.

Adults are key to making the best of the potential of the outdoor provision for children.

The EYFS reminds us that the crucial element to best support and extend young children's learning outdoors is the presence of knowledgeable adults who are sensitive to and respond to children's needs and whom children can trust.

The EYFS tells us that adults should:

- offer a range of experiences and resources which are regularly monitored and refreshed to keep them safe and stimulating;
- tune in to the children's interests and interact with them to support and extend their learning and development, jointly engaging in problem-solving and sustained shared thinking;
- respond to observed interests and plan new materials and experiences within the environment that reflect them;
- monitor materials, children's involvement and their own involvement with children to ensure they offer relevant experiences;
- provide materials that reflect diversity in order to avoid stereotypical images or approaches;
- evaluate their provision to ensure that everything that is provided is of the highest quality;
- support children's confidence in themselves and their developing skills as they tackle new experiences and develop a sense of what they can do and what they will be able to do as they practise and meet the challenges in the environment.

All of these points are equally relevant for the outdoor learning environment and will help practitioners to reflect on the planning for using technology outdoors with young children.

Starting points in using technology outdoors

In beginning to use technology outdoors it is best to start from something you and the children are already familiar with. Digital cameras are a good starting point as most practitioners are using these at least for record-keeping purposes.

Whatever camera you have, it should be possible to share it with the children, or for them to have their own camera. It is such a useful tool for young children to use that it would be a shame to miss out on the opportunities it can provide.

Choosing a digital camera

The way you choose to use a digital camera will probably depend on funding issues. If you have raised money and saved hard for this precious tool, then you are going to feel more nervous about putting it in the hands of children. In this case:

- Take out insurance. Our local camera shop offers three-year insurance on cameras we purchase from them. This includes accidental damage (even being dropped by children!) and they offer a full repair or replacement guarantee.
- Buy a camera that is suitable for your purpose. There are plastic-coated cameras on the market (see Appendix 1) that withstand quite a lot of heavy use from children! The camera is easy for young children to use and the images can instantly be seen through the camera display or through connection to a computer without specialist software. This camera does, however, require batteries rather than having an integral rechargeable battery and the quality of images is low.
- If you go for a higher-quality adult camera that includes an integral rechargeable battery (always best to go for this option if you can: saves on batteries and is easy to recharge), then add a long thick strap so that children can carry the camera safely. Look for a camera that has few buttons if possible, and one with a good-sized display screen. If you are sharing the camera with children, then try to buy one that can record video with sound so that you have use of this facility.

Introducing a camera to children

- Choose a place indoors where the camera can be sited, somewhere it is kept throughout a session and show practitioners and children know where to collect it and return it to when they need it. A tray on a cupboard top at children's height works well.
- Have an adult near this space at first while the children are getting used to sharing the camera.
- Introduce the camera to all the children. Demonstrate how the first thing that you do is wear the safety strap. Talk about the camera with the children, asking them about their own knowledge and experience of cameras. Emphasise the delicate nature of the camera and how they should take care of it. I ask the children to imagine something delicate they have held (like a glass or a small animal) and ask them to hold the camera just as carefully.
- Demonstrate the least you need to do to take a picture and to view it on the camera,

i.e. removing the lens cap, seeing through the display and selecting your shot, clicking the button to take the picture, pressing the button to see the picture in the camera display.

- Model using the camera for a purpose, safely. Talk through your actions so children know why and how you are using the camera.
- Teach individual children on a need-to-know basis. Some children with enough experience, at around four years old, will be able to get as far as deleting pictures from the camera and attaching the camera to a computer, selecting the photos they want to print and printing them out.
- Encourage the children to help each other use the camera, describing what the buttons do. Introduce the correct vocabulary; it is a good opportunity for developing communication and language.

A note about learning

The ideas here are not always linked to specific stages of development or areas of learning. They are intended as starting points that can be used to help stimulate thinking when you are observing and planning. They can be used entirely flexibly so that they can be adapted to fit with the age group, interests and learning of the children that you are working with.

Once the children are familiar with the camera and know where to fetch it from and return it to, start using it outside. There are limitless ideas for using a camera outside, so think back to all that has been written previously about the benefits of outdoor play and plan to support and develop these features of outdoor play through using a digital camera. Here are a few ideas:

Children using a digital camera

- Ask children to take a photo of their most favourite place in the outdoor area, or the place they like the least! Print these off and put them on the snack table indoors for developing CLLD and PSED. Invite dialogue with open questions or through commenting on the photos, such as, 'That's an interesting photo. What is it about that place that you like?', or 'That looks like a very dark place. Do you go inside sometimes? What is it like in there?'
- Children enjoy photographing their friends, and they will often do this spontaneously, which is not surprising when we think of the photographs we often choose to take. Make a photo album with the children of each child playing outside. Use this to support PSRN, CLLD and PSED. Ask the children to mark off on a register when they have taken a photo of a friend playing outside. Use this for counting how many photos have been taken, and how many still need to be taken. Support children in printing the completed collection and help them make an album: 'How many pages will we need? How shall we lay the photos out?' Bring the album outside and share it with the children, discussing what they and their friends like to do outside.
- The children could take photographs of their collections of natural objects, leading a spontaneous playful activity into a more developed experience of art. Share the photographs they take through the camera display and ask the children if they

want to rearrange their collections to make a different picture. Share postcards or images on the Internet of the work of artists who use natural materials such as Andy Goldsworthy. Gradually add paper or hoops to work on or around, encouraging the children to see and create shapes and mixtures of colours in their collections. The children could photograph the work in progress and make a display indoors, or laminate the photographs and display them outside to encourage further work. These experiences could support CLLD, CD or PSRN, depending on the children's focus and the child and adult interactions.

Figure 5.1 Look how this child has enjoyed working with pairs of objects!

Children using video

Children need a great deal of experience of using a video camera and using the camera software experimentally before they are ready to use it for a purpose. Children as young as three can use the movie-maker camera (see Appendix 1 and Appendix 5).

Encourage this period of experimenting without feeling the need for the experience to be more developed. Observe the children's use of the camera and software and gradually lead their investigations into making small movies together.

- Some children enjoy 'playing' in front of the camera, popping in and out of a box, role-playing a character, dressing up or coming in and out of doors. Others will like to be the 'directors', telling the actors what to do and enjoying seeing the effects of their filming.
- Record visits out. Children can each take their own tiny clip of their visit out, for pond dipping, for example, and these can be put together easily as a single 'movie' with the movie-maker camera software (or use Photo Story). Some children will have videoed a drain, others a hub cap, others a friend, and some may have videoed

the creatures in the pond! Each child choosing what they want to video creates a truly shared story about the visit.

Hot tip!

The movie-maker camera requires a button to be depressed for taking video. It is very difficult for young children to continually hold down this button. To get around this, click the self-timer button, click the video button and release. Then the end of a ticking sound will signal that the video has started, the child can now video and it is only when they click the video button again that the video will stop recording.

Adults using a digital camera

- Photograph children's physical achievements, add to their record books or share through display.
- Photograph collaborations to reinforce positive personal and social developments.
- Photograph plants that children are growing, to show the sequence of the various stages of planting and growing. Laminate the photos and clip them to a fence or hang them outside by the planting.
- Take photographs on zoom from a raised area. Give the children binoculars and see if they can find what the photograph is of. This will encourage close observation and identification of natural objects and spaces in the environment.

Video cameras can extend the uses of photography still further:

- Use video to record children's play outdoors, picking up on things they may not notice at the time, such as the shadows they are creating or the outward splash of a puddle. Watch the video together inside (on a screen or IWB if you have one) and use discussion to support PSED, K&U and CLLD.
- Record children's role play for encouraging children's storytelling and links with developing literacy.

Outdoor wireless cameras:

- Outdoor wireless cameras can be positioned in places of interest and picked up through a monitor indoors. Through this the children can see the natural world more closely without disturbing it, for example, capturing birds nesting, or it can be focused on a play area, encouraging children inside to be stimulated by what is going on or to reflect on outdoor experiences.
- A television monitor or plasma screen in the front entrance can pick up on the outdoor webcam and enable and support talk between parents, carers and their children. How much easier this is than children having to answer the question, 'What did you do today?', away from the context of their learning.

There are so many ideas for using still and moving images: see Appendix 2 for further ideas.

Using technology outdoors: what works?

Defunct technology

Defunct technology fits really well into the outdoors. You need a very large box, prefer-ably on wheels. Fill this with old technology that no longer works, for example, printers, keyboards, mice, headphones, microphones, webcams, remote controls, phones, digital watches. Put the box alongside other resources such as large blocks, crates or cardboard boxes.

Figure 5.2

Have conversations with the children about this being old technology that no longer works and that is why it is all right for us to use it in play. Also regularly check the equipment for health and safety (we cut off the wires from keyboards and take out any loose parts from printers), and observe the children at play to make sure they are using the equipment safely.

Make sure there is plenty of space for children to take things out of the box and to build into their creations.

This box of defunct technology works even better if the children have regular access to 'making' materials that they are used to using and know where to find. These can be provided in a trolley that can be quickly wheeled outside and might include: tape, bulldog clips, cloths, collage materials, including natural ones collected with the children, pegs, rope, small buckets, paint rollers, tubes, chalk, notepads, clipboards and pencils.

The obvious advantage of using defunct technology is that it does not matter what happens to it! It can break and be thrown away or rained on and dried out. Children incorporate old technology into their play with ease. They may build a spaceship from cardboard boxes, taping keyboards to their 'control area' and adding remotes and printers while they set to work, or they may lay the tools out on top of blocks, buy and sell them and take them away in prams or carts.

Figure 5.3

This play will spark all kinds of dialogue, between children and children and between adults and children, around the uses and nature of technology. By talking about technology children can build their cultural awareness of the place that different technologies take in their lives. This is a different kind of learning from building children's ICT skills or using ICT to support learning, but learning that I think is becoming increasingly important if children are going to be able to harness the real power of technologies in the world they are growing up in today.

Remote controls and programmable toys

There are all kinds of programmable toys and remote control vehicles on the market today; I have added a couple of our favourites to the resources listed in Appendix 1.

Beebots are programmable toys. They resemble small bugs and you can buy clip-on covers for them so that they can be transformed into different identities. They have simple controls that children can quickly work out by trial and error, by talking through and by being shown.

Figure 5.4

Figure 5.5

These are excellent for use outside, where the children can take full advantage of the space. They are not wholly robust and when using them outdoors it is sensible to put them on a mat or large cardboard or plywood sheets. There are many ready-made resources that you can buy for Beebots, including roadways and tunnels and pulleys, but making resources with the children, or combining familiar resources that are already in your environment, will give the children a greater sense of ownership.

Manage the Beebots either by keeping them in a box, bringing them outside and putting them near something appropriate, like the blocks, or have an indoor space where the children know they can go and collect them and bring them outside when they want.

- Try making cardboard box beehives for the Beebots to live in. Flowers in pots can be put nearby for the bees to come out and visit. Or cover them and call them vehicles and make cardboard box garages for the Beebots to be steered into.
- Combining the Beebots with other materials lends itself to all kinds of collaborative problem-solving as tunnels and bridges and towers are made for the Beebot to travel around.

Figure 5.6

The child in Figure 5.7 found a Beebot could climb up slopes. He wanted to see if it could pull things up a slope and knew where to find string and a Duplo truck. Later he added animals to his truck until he found it was too hard for the Beebot to pull and he had to help it on its journey.

Remote control bugs or vehicles come in many forms. One of the most robust are Duplo remote control vehicles. These remotes operate on different radio frequencies, so one child's control won't operate another child's vehicle. They can be kept in a box to be used inside or out, and there are some small parts, so it is useful to have a tray outside that the children can put the parts into as they bring them out of the box.

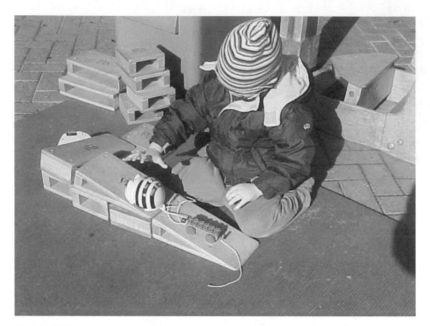

Figure 5.7

Figure 5.8

These vehicles can be used on many different levels, making them suitable for even the youngest of children. They have screwdrivers to combine the parts, encouraging children's fine motor development. The vehicles can be driven quite far from the remotes, making them fun for racing against each other. They lend themselves to collaboration and problem-solving as children steer them around obstacles or deliberately make them bump into them! Play can support PSRN and CLLD and PSED.

Figure 5.9

Role-play boxes

One of the practitioners' roles outside is to observe children's play closely, to evaluate their learning and to plan for their next steps.

We can support children's socio-dramatic play more immediately if we have role-play boxes that already contain the materials that could support a particular role-play.

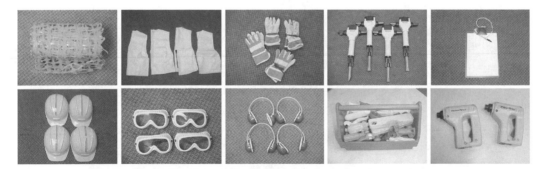

Figure 5.10 Builders' role-play box

By making role-play boxes in advance, it's possible to think through the resources that you want to add to develop CLLD, PSRN and ICT. Here are a few ideas for the kinds of technology that could be added to role-play boxes for outdoor use:

- torches
- play drills
- timers
- walkie-talkies

- mobile phones
- defunct or toy cameras
- digital till
- bar code scanner
- sound recorders or voice changers
- laptop case
- calculators
- headphones
- old remote controls
- make labels using ICT with children, e.g. 'Post Office', or 'Builders at Work!'.

There are many other technologies that can be used to support, extend and add to outdoor learning. Use the web links in Appendix 3 to gather further ideas for ways of developing uses of these resources. Here are just a few. Observe children's play carefully and use the following ideas to build on their play and their interests.

Digital microscope or visualiser

- Connect the outdoors with indoors by investigating found objects. Mini-beasts can also be carefully taken inside and seen more closely through a digital microscope or visualiser. Both will take still and moving images of the creatures. The photographs can be added to the art area to encourage children to look closely and have a go at drawing what they have seen. Remember to use it as an opportunity to teach care of living creatures.

Figure 5.11

Tape recorders, CD players and MP3 players

Look out for the increasing number of ways in which sound can be recorded and heard that are coming on to the market. MP3 players have considerably advanced the portability of recording and recorded sound. These players gradually find their way into the education catalogues, so send away for these free catalogues (see suppliers' contacts in Appendix 1) to keep in touch with the new technologies that are becoming available.

- Increase the children's opportunities for hearing songs and rhymes and listening to stories by adding a tape recorder and a collection of books in a quiet space outside. Children love to listen to these under a tree or in a rocking boat!
- Record sounds and take the children on a sound hunt. Ask them where they have heard that sound before and what could possibly make that sound. This is a really good listening game that will help children to discriminate sounds, an important development towards becoming literate.

Music mats, microphones and sound recorders

There are many kinds of sound recorders on the market. Ones that are similar to free-standing microphones are excellent for adding to outdoor play (see Appendix 1).

- Make a stage or music area. Add a selection from music mats, karaoke machines, sound recorders or play microphones that have sound effects. Children will enjoy singing rhymes and songs that they know together. This largely takes the form of role-play and can encourage children to have a voice (see Chapter 4).
- Record small chunks of dialogue while children are at play. Later, indoors, play these back together to reflect on their experiences.
- Record children's storytelling. Play these back together later when the children have a wider audience of friends or the whole class, asking them first if they would like to share their story. This will build on their communication, language and literacy skills.

Conclusion

In this chapter we have looked at the value of outdoor learning and how to under-pin this with using technologies in young children's play. The examples above show us that technology enhances and adds to children's traditional forms of learning outdoors. It has a transforming and powerful effect, allowing for greater opportunities to extend, reflect upon and discuss experiences. I hope the chapter has given you some ideas of developing ICT outdoors in your own practice. The idea is not to offer all of these experiences all of the time, but to make the subject manageable and to offer high-quality ICT experiences enriched through sensitive and knowledgeable adult support.

6 ICT and role play

Rachel Ager

While playing children can express fears and re-live anxious experiences. They can try things out, solve problems and be creative and can take risks and use trial and error to find things out.

Children who are allowed to play with resources and equipment before using them to solve a problem are more likely to solve the problem more successfully.

The Early Years Foundation Stage (DCSF 2008)

Introduction

Role play is a vital element in the learning environment as it engages children in play which reflects their lives and gives them the opportunity to experience and recreate roles, emotions and relationships. Good-quality role play gives children the opportunity to make sense of the world in which we live and most importantly it helps them to make sense of the increasingly technological world in which we now live. They can handle the ICT tools that they see in the world about them, experiment and take control of them and learn about these objects and their place in the world. Role play can give children the opportunity to take control of familiar ICT tools which they may not normally be allowed to use unsupervised. For instance, though nearly all homes now have a mobile phone, children are usually not allowed to use these unsupervised. Parents lock mobile phones to ensure that their children do not make accidental calls, run up large bills inadvertently or make nuisance calls.

In the kitchen

A kitchen has been set up with a range of wooden equipment including sink, washing machine, plates, bowls, knives, forks and spoons, and a variety of food. There is a variety of real, though not functioning, props including a clock, kettle and baby monitor and a mobile phone and cordless phone.

One child is ironing when another child hands the mobile phone to her. She carries on ironing whilst she talks on the phone, using her elbow when necessary to steady the ironing.

Figure 6.1

Later she takes the phone and, studying the Chinese takeaway menu carefully, confidently orders chicken.

Figure 6.2

Another child is using the cordless phone. As he chats on the phone he makes a space for the telephone's base unit on the counter. So that he can use both hands to do this, he tucks the phone between his chin and shoulder and carries on talking whilst he makes the space he needs.

Figure 6.3

When telephones are added to a role-play area children are quick to incorporate them into their play and it is obvious from observing the children described above that phones are used regularly within their homes, although it is very unlikely that they are allowed to use them except under close supervision.

Role play can also give children the confidence to begin to use new ICT tools with which they are less familiar and which they might otherwise be reluctant to use. Through role play, practitioners can encourage children to use the equipment appropriately and safely and they can encourage conversation about how the equipment works using the correct technical language. When planning role play it is important not only to consider what technology the children have at home but to understand whether the children are allowed to use the technology and for what purpose.

Planning role play

When children enter the Foundation Stage their ICT knowledge, skills and understanding are usually already well developed and many children are technically competent and confident users of the variety of technologies which they come into contact with on a regular basis. For instance they may be able to use the Sky+ remote control to navigate the on-screen menus to access the television programme they want to watch and to record it, and they can come back later and again navigate the on-screen menus to replay it. They may make phone calls using a mobile phone, or use it to take photographs and know that these can be shared with others. They may even be able to access photos stored on the phone. Children are beginning to understand that ICT can be used for a range of purposes such as communication and entertainment and are beginning to use it for these purposes. It is vital that practitioners value and understand these developing competencies so they plan for challenging and stimulating role play with clear learning intentions that build on what children already know and can do.

Planning for role play, like all effective planning, will be largely informed by discussions with other practitioners and parents and by ongoing observations and assessments of the children.

Practitioners need to develop a clear understanding of children's developing ICT competencies, in particular in relation to the vast range of everyday technologies with which children come into contact. Practitioners not only need to value the competencies that children develop at home; they also need to appreciate the links that these have with the ICT competencies that they are trying to develop in children while they are in the setting. A child's ability to use a Sky remote control or play on a PlayStation might not seem relevant to practitioners when they are planning experiences aimed at developing a child's ICT competencies, but they need to appreciate that a competent user of a PlayStation may well be more competent and confident when learning to navigate new software and may well take less time to learn to use the software.

How developed a child's ICT competencies are will vary and this will in part be due to the access that they have had to technology at home. Their ICT competence and confidence will also be dependent on the attitude of family members to the child as a user of technology. Research has shown that children from homes with less technology will be more competent users of the technology if the family has an enthusiastic attitude to the technologies and a positive attitude to the children's use of that technology.

Such children will be exposed to a wider range of activities and experiences involving ICT than a child from 'technology rich' homes where the family restrict the child's access to the technology or are less interested in involving young children in ICT-based activities and experiences. A child's ability to use ICT depends, therefore, not only on whether the technology is available in the home, but on the degree of access permitted by parents.

If practitioners are to develop an understanding of children's ICT competencies when they enter the setting, they need to ask more than what ICT is available in the home. They need to ascertain what access the children have had to the technology and to understand the nature of ICT activities and experiences the children have had at home. Research has shown that, far from engaging in discussions with parents about children's ICT experiences at home, practitioners have a very limited knowledge of children's ICT competencies when they enter the setting and often do not value the experiences that the children have had. They are therefore not in a position to build on these skills. Once practitioners understand each child's developing ICT competencies and understand the links with the competencies that the child is developing at home, they are in a position to plan challenging role play which builds on what children know and can already do.

They will also be able to consider how the role-play experience can be adapted for individuals or groups of children, including children with specific needs such as those whose first language is not English.

During the planning process practitioners should consider other factors which will affect the quality of the role play. These include:

- the children's own life experiences and knowledge;
- how the children will be involved in the setting up of the role play area in the setting;
- the attitudes of the adults and their involvement in the play;
- the space available;
- whether it will be indoors and/or outdoors;
- the time available in the setting's daily routine;
- whether there is the opportunity for the role play to develop over time;
- the quality and appropriateness of the resources.

The quality and appropriateness of resources

Settings should provide a role-play area with materials and props that reflect the children's family lives, their communities and the world in which they live. The quality and appropriateness of resources directly affects the quality of the role play within a role-play area. However, this does not mean that it is necessary to go out and purchase the seemingly never-ending array of technology that we might consider necessary to equip a role-play area in order that it accurately reflects the world in which we live. It is necessary, however, to have a range of different types of resources, each of which is valuable in its own way. Resources will include:

- real items of technology that work, such as digital cameras;
- real items of technology that no longer work, such as kettles;

- toy technologies that simulate the working of the real technology in some way, such as a microwave oven with lights that turn on and a revolving turntable;
- toy technologies, such as a wooden washing machine;
- technologies that the children have made, such as a photocopier made from cardboard boxes, plastic bottle lids and silver foil.

Each of these types of resources can add something unique to a role-play area.

Real technologies

Integrating real technology into role play gives children the opportunity to explore technologies and develop their understanding of how they work and why we would want to use them and use them within a supportive and unthreatening environment. As the children grow in competence and confidence, and as the role play develops over time, the children can begin to use these technologies for a real purpose within the context of the role-play situation. For instance, a photographic studio can be enhanced by the introduction of a real digital camera that allows the children to take photographs of the other children, which can then be framed and 'sold'.

The photographic studio, I

Three children pose for a photograph (taken by a fourth child) in a portrait studio. As the photographer takes the first photograph the young boy pulls a face. He is reprimanded by the photographer and asked to smile. The photographer takes a second photograph and tells the children she has finished. The teacher intervenes and asks her whether she has checked the photograph to make sure she is happy with it. She then does so and discovers that the girl in the photograph had her eyes shut. The three children pose again and the photographer reminds them to smile, look this way and keep their eyes open! She takes the photograph and this time checks it unprompted.

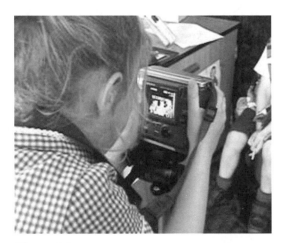

Figure 6.4

Through the introduction of a real camera the quality of the role play has been enhanced. There is much more of a need to remind those posing for their photograph to 'sit still' and 'look this way' if a child is taking a real photograph, and equally there is much more of a need to sit appropriately if you know your photograph is really going to be taken. Through the role play the children are learning how to use the camera appropriately and also learning and developing the language and behaviours associated with this.

Toy technologies

However, it is often not necessary or desirable to use real technologies within a role-play area. When using real technologies the children can become too focused on getting the technology to work rather than role playing its use and through this role play developing an understanding of how and why we use that particular technology. Instead the role-play area can be equipped with toy technologies. These may have few or no working parts, such as a wooden kettle, or they may 'work' in some way, such as an electronic kettle that has an on/off button, which when switched on lights up and the kettle makes a water boiling noise. Toys that 'work' may enhance the role play and prompt actions and reactions from the children.

At the café

A four-year-old child is 'making' a pizza out of play dough 'in the kitchen'. She puts it into the micro-wave and presses the 'On' button. The light inside comes on and the turn-table starts to rotate but the pizza is too large to turn. She switches the microwave oven off, takes out the pizza, trims a bit off the edge, puts the pizza back into the microwave oven and switches it on again. The pizza is still too big and she repeats the process twice more before it is small enough for the pizza.

Figure 6.5

Problem solving: The toy microwave oven had a turntable that rotated and because of this any food item placed inside needs to be small enough to allow the turntable to rotate freely. As the 'pizza' was too large it was necessary to make it smaller, and one method of solving the problem was to trim it a bit at a time until it 'fitted'.

Figure 6.6

Just as toy technologies that 'work' can enhance role play, on other occasions the role play is better facilitated by non-'working' versions. Children can become distracted by the lights and noise of toy technologies and sometimes the role play flows better without too many of them.

Made technologies

Technologies that the children have made make excellent props for role play and these should in no way be seen as second best. In some respects they can be more valuable than other types of resources. Children can and will make anything from 'photo-copiers' to 'cash registers' to equip a role-play area. They will be particularly keen to make these if they have been involved in planning for and setting up the area from the outset. Not only will the role-play area and the play within it be enhanced by the addition of these props, but the children's understanding of the technologies can be developed by the practitioner through appropriate questioning and dialogue during the making process. Alternatively, by observing children construct the resources a practitioner is able to develop a greater understanding of what the child understands about the technology. For instance, if a child is making a toaster, does he make a slot for the toast and does it have a plug so it can be plugged in?

The garden centre, I

During a visit to their local garden centre a group of children took digital photographs of various pieces of technology. Back at the setting they use the photos to decide what technology they want to include in the garden centre role-play area as they set it up. They decide they need a till for the café and one child decides to make this. She studies the photograph carefully and selects an appropriate box, which she covers with tin foil. She then cuts squares of paper and writes numbers on them and, after consulting the photograph, she sticks them on the appropriate place on the till. She cuts out more squares and in these writes the names of the foods sold in the café: coffee, Ribena, etc.

Figure 6.7

Figure 6.8

The children's involvement in setting up the role-play area

If children have been involved in setting up a role-play area the quality of the play is likely to show greater involvement and higher levels of engagement. The children are more likely to have an understanding and expectation of how to use the role-play area and are more likely to use it with care. The most effective way to stimulate the children's involvement in setting up a role-play area is for the children to visit the setting that they wish to create, to see this in action, to use some of the technology if possible and to be supported in asking questions and discussing what they see. On the visit the children could use digital photography or video to record what they see and do. These pictures can then be used back at the setting to remind the children of the visit and to help them decide how they would like to set up the role-play area and what props they want to include. The photographs can also be used by the children as models when making props, and they can be referred back to by practitioners and children as the role play develops over time.

However, it is not always possible for children to make such a visit. In this case a practitioner could visit a 'real-world' setting that will act as a context for role play and record it using digital photography or video. They may want to take a class toy with them to join them on the visit, 'Barnaby Bear style'. The children can then be shown the video and photographs and ask questions of the practitioner who made the visit. In addition it may be possible to have a visitor or visitors come to the setting and then children can be given the opportunity to use some of the technology and ask questions.

The garden centre, 2

During their visit to the garden centre the children took digital photographs and video. As soon as they got back to the setting they looked at these and discussed what they had seen and done. They began to consider how their garden centre was going to be set up and what props they needed. Some of the children then moved to the workshop area and started making a chip and pin machine and a cash register.

Figure 6.9

Figure 6.10

The attitude and involvement of adults

The attitudes of the adults and their involvement in the play are key influences on the quality of the role play that ensues. Adults engaged in role play can and should model behaviours, including how to use the available technologies appropriately and safely and any rules that should govern our behaviour. They can engage children in conversation and discussions about how things work and why we use them, and they can model use of the correct vocabulary, including technical vocabulary. This may be of particular importance to those children whose first language is not English or who sign or use other forms of communication.

Open-ended questions are important tools and in helping children to understand how technology works and why we use it. For example, 'What would happen here if I pressed this button?', 'How can we make this programmable toy move to here?', 'Can you find a way to record a message?', 'What could we use the walkie-talkie for?', 'How does the metal detector work?' and 'What does the microwave oven do?' The practitioner should involve herself in children's discussions and encourage them to tell each other what they have found out or to describe their experiences. In doing so, children will rehearse and reflect on their knowledge and practise new vocabulary. When using technology it is important that the practitioner provides a positive role model. They must show that they understand the need for technology and value its use. Children seeing this will develop a positive attitude to the technologies they encounter, they will be motivated to use and understand these technologies and hopefully be empowered by technology throughout their lives.

At the fish and chip shop

The fish and chip shop was set up following a visit to the local fish and chip shop. There is a 'deep fat fryer', chip basket, plastic fish and chips, a till and a phone.

Figure 6.11

The practitioner answers the phone and hands it to a child, saying, 'I'll just hand you over to the manager.' When the child hands the phone back, the practitioner asks, 'Is it an order?' The child replies, 'Yes', and the practitioner enquires, 'What do the people want?' The child replies, 'Fish fingers', and the practitioner responds, 'Do they want any chips?'

At the greengrocer's

A greengrocer's shop has been set up. On the counter there is a toy telephone and cash register and a real calculator. An adult comes up to the shop and asks for a cauliflower, which the 'greengrocer' gets for her. She then asks for two carrots and asks the greengrocer if she can write a list of everything she buys because she forgets and then she forgets to put them in her soup. When she has everything she needs, she asks the greengrocer, 'Can you add that up for me and see how much I owe you?' She gently pushes the calculator in her direction. The greengrocer pushes the buttons on the calculator and says '2'. The adult asks if that is £2 or 2p, and on being told that it is 2p she pays for her vegetables and the greengrocer puts the money in the till.

Figure 6.12

Figure 6.13

Indoors and outdoors

It is important that role-play areas when appropriate are set up outdoors as well as indoors: for instance, a builders' yard or a police speed trap. By having two linked role-play areas it is possible to make to make links between the indoor and outdoor environments. This will also encourage children to move spontaneously between the two environments – for instance, in a garden centre.

The garden centre, 3

The children visited the local garden centre and were involved in setting up the role play in the setting. They set up the plant shop and pet shop outside and a café inside.

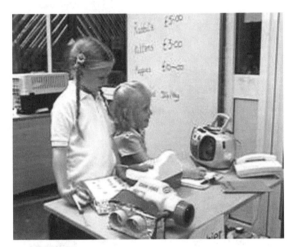

Figure 6.14

Figure 6.15

Police speed trap

The local police have visited the setting and discussed why they use a mobile speed camera and how it works. The children then made their own speed camera, which they use outside to check the speed of those children riding the tricycles and other wheeled toys, and issue tickets as appropriate.

Figure 6.16

Figure 6.17

To learn without failure

Practitioners should plan challenging and stimulating role play that builds on what children already know and can do. It is also important that children are provided with a secure environment with effective and sensitive adult support in which they can take risks and make mistakes without fear of failure. It is therefore important that children are given time to explore new technologies and learn to use them before being expected to use them for a common purpose.

As adults, if we want to use a new piece of technology such as a digital camera, we take the time to 'play' with it, exploring how it works until we are confident that we can use it. During this time we only use it when it doesn't matter how successful the outcome is. It is important that we give children the time that they need to explore any new piece of technology that we introduce to the setting. If this is a digital camera it may be that we allow them to use the camera for their own purpose, in other words to take photographs of things of their own choosing, or we may set up a simple scenario that allows the children to explore the use of the camera and develop the confidence and competence to use it successfully.

At the seaside

The setting has just bought some new digital cameras. They have been exploring many aspects of holidaying at the seaside and so the practitioner has painted a façade on a door, into which the children can look to have their photograph taken. The cameras are available for the children to use to take these photographs, and as they do so they develop their understanding of how to use the cameras. With each photograph they take, their competence increases.

Figure 6.18

The photographic studio, 2

In the photographic studio described, the camera was set up on a tripod so that the 'photographer' did not have to worry about framing the photograph and could concentrate on interacting with those posing for their photograph. Those children who were not yet confident or competent users of the camera could take on the role of photographer successfully. The quality of the role play was not affected by the children's ability to use the camera. All children could use the camera without fear of failure.

Figure 6.19

Through role play children can learn how to use the technologies available, but we do not want a child's competence in using the technology to affect the quality of their role play, or for them to feel that they may not manage the technology. Practitioners need to consider ways in which children can be supported in their confidence in using technology and where the possibility of failure is reduced or eliminated.

Supporting Communication, Language and Literacy and Mathematical Development

When ICT is incorporated seamlessly into role play it can serve to promote and enable meaningful communication and give children the opportunity to use and develop their mathematical knowledge, skills and understanding in practical contexts. The children can use the technology purposefully within their play.

Under the sea

Figure 6.20

'The ocean bed' is a large tray filled with sand in an 'under the sea' role-play area. The boat is in the outside area out of sight of the ocean bed. Three children take on the role of deep sea divers and search for treasure on the sea bed using metal detectors. As they find each item, they use a walkie-talkie to relay the information to children in a boat, who make a list of the finds.

The three divers negotiate the roles they each will take, deciding who will use the two metal detectors and who will use the walkie-talkie. At the same time the boat crew successfully negotiate their roles, deciding who will use the walkie-talkie, who will use the clipboard and who will row the boat. As they begin to use the metal detectors, the

Figure 6.21

divers discuss what they might find with anticipation. With each new find, the walkie-talkie is used to relay the information to the boat crew and the information is written down on the clipboard. They attempt to sound out each word, 'silver spoon', 'gold ring' . . ., and collectively decide the spelling as the scribe writes.

The builder's yard

A builder's yard has been set up outside. They have an office fully equipped with toy telephone, toy cash register, toy walkie-talkies, laptop, pencils, pens and sticky notes. A short distance away a variety of bricks and tools are available for sale and for the 'builders' to use. The laptop has been set up with the programme 2email so that the class teacher can 'send' emails from customers to the site office, to which the 'office staff' must respond. Since the role-play area was set up the week before, a Pixie programmable toy has been added. The children decided they needed this to take the messages from the office to the builders.

Figure 6.22

Two boys realise there are unopened emails to be read. Supported by the teacher, they open the first email and read it. This is from Bob the builder, who wants to know if anyone is available to help him build a house. The children decide they are too busy to help him today. Bob will have to wait until Monday. They type their reply, 'We can hlp on Mundy', and send this to Bob. The two boys open the second email. It is from Ben the builder who wants to buy 20 bricks. They write on a sticky note, 'Ben 20 brics'. They pass this to another child, who puts it on Pixie and then programs the toy to take the message over to the brick store.

Figure 6.23

Health and safety

General health and safety awareness relating to ICT should form part of children's learning about ICT, and the usual guidance should be followed when deciding which pieces of equipment the children use and whether they need to be supervised directly by an adult. The only additional guidance that should be followed is that, where children are using real technology that doesn't work within a role-play area, the power cable should be removed so the children are not tempted to plug it in.

Conclusion

Role play helps children make sense of the world and it must therefore reflect the technological world in which we live. As the above examples illustrate, well-planned role play encourages cooperative play and gives the children opportunities to use language, develop literacy and numeracy skills and to learn without failure. Technology has been seamlessly incorporated into this role play and, while the children are developing their understanding of how the walkie-talkies, metal detectors, email and digital cameras work, the real importance of the tools is that they serve to promote and enable purposeful and meaningful communication. The children are using the ICT tools for their own purpose within their play.

7 The use of ICT with children with special needs

Julia Coles

Introduction

At Rowan Gate Primary School, a school for children aged between 3 and 11 years with a range of learning difficulties including autistic spectrum disorders and profound and multiple learning difficulties, we have a strong belief in the power that ICT can have to open up and enrich a curriculum that might otherwise be denied to our pupils.

Underpinning much of our work, as in almost any Early Years Foundation Stage (EYFS) setting across the country, are the EYFS Principles and a belief that, in order for children to 'find out about and identify the uses of technology in their everyday lives', they need to:

- explore, investigate and operate these technologies;
- discover and observe their uses within the setting and outside it;
- discover, practise, rehearse and repeat the uses of these everyday technologies through role play with toys that simulate the real technologies;
- discuss the use of these technologies, including the enormous impact they have on our everyday lives;
- learn the correct vocabulary associated with everyday technologies (hearing adults model the use of this language);
- dismantle these technologies to investigate what is inside them.

(Northamptonshire County Council 2003)

In the early stages of establishing our own vision as a lead school for Early Years ICT, it was necessary to consider the question 'What do children learn when they are using a full range of technology?' and this question is as relevant to children with complex needs and difficulties as it is to those who are of average ability or, indeed, those who are already demonstrating high ability.

They learn:

- concentration
- making choices
- ability to transfer and apply skills

- problem solving/creative thinking
- communication
- creativity
- social skills: sharing, turn taking, collaborating
- exploration
- persistence
- following instructions
- questioning
- hand–eye co-ordination
- understanding of shape and space
- cause and effect
- mouse control
- names of parts of a computer
- use of language (e.g. positional).

Unlocking the curriculum

The role that ICT can play in making the Early Years curriculum – indeed, any curriculum – meaningful to children with Special Educational Needs is a hugely important one. ICT ensures that all children regardless of ability or difficulty can be included in appropriate and meaningful learning opportunities. It helps to promote an inclusive environment where all children in the setting can participate and engage in significant learning experiences.

ICT plays an important role within the education of children, particularly those with Special Educational Needs, as it enables them, through various means, to access a broad and balanced curriculum, one that they might otherwise be denied. Some children may have difficulties in communicating their needs and wants so through the use of communication aids such as Big Mack and Go Talk (see Appendix 1, Software and resources) children can be given the opportunity to make requests and use simple greetings during circle time.

Many children with quite complex physical needs might not be able to access simple equipment due to physical impairment. Through ICT it is possible to provide the means by which children can have access to equipment, for example, a toy in which a green orang-utan is controlled to play a guitar is switch-enabled – no fiddling with a tiny on/off button – children can press the switch (about the size of a side plate) and they are able to operate the toy without adult intervention.

In 'Calculating the Digital Divide' (2002) Madden states that 'One of the primary driving factors behind people's use of technologies is relevance.' I believe this to be particularly true when related to children with Special Educational Needs. If a learning experience that utilises technology is of greater relevance to a child, then this will motivate and inspire them to explore or enquire to a greater degree than if the task or activity has no relevance. A great deal of learning can be initiated and motivated through programmes which include sound, images of themselves or images that are of particular relevance to themselves (e.g. *The Tweenies* or *Teletubbies* and, more recently, *Cars* or *The Incredibles*). Visual, Auditory and Kinaesthetic learning styles (VAK) are all promoted through the use of ICT, thus meeting a wide range of learning styles almost irrespective of ability.

Figure 7.1

I will endeavour to show in this chapter how ICT has served to enhance the learning experiences of children with significant learning difficulties. However, I believe that many of these activities would be equally at home in mainstream settings.

First it is necessary to consider how technology assists in working towards our learning outcomes or goals. Here are some of the possible benefits that mainstream and special needs Early Years teachers in Northamptonshire felt might result from the use of ICT and computers:

- makes the curriculum more accessible;
- acts as a motivator to many children;
- links real-life situations to learning;
- makes learning meaningful and relevant;
- can encourage interaction (e.g. walkie-talkies);
- allows children to succeed (removing barriers to learning);
- allows children to transfer skills;
- is a means of managing children's learning;
- has the possibility of parental involvement.

Making the curriculum more accessible

So much of the ICT equipment that we use in school helps to give children improved accessibility in terms of the curriculum. A prime example of this is the interactive whiteboard and the power it has to make a difference to children's learning. At Rowan Gate Primary School each class has access to its own interactive whiteboard and projector. Previously we had been proud of the fact that in many classes children had access to touch-screen monitors with the classroom PC. However, where children had co-ordination or physical difficulties the monitors often proved more frustrating than enabling, as children struggled to touch very specific areas of the monitor screen. By introducing the interactive whiteboards we saw an improvement in the opportunities for children to access software, as they were not relying on fine motor skills but were able to put their gross motor skills to good use. We had deliberately chosen interactive whiteboards that responded to touching the screen with the hand (or any implement) rather than using a specific stylus or 'pen'. This eliminated the need for children to learn the skill of holding a pen. When the whiteboards were installed we aimed to site all the boards so that a child who was able to stand would then be able to touch almost all of the screen area.

Problem: For some children who were reliant on a standing frame or wheelchair, the physical equipment tended to limit the extent or area of the board that the children could access.

Solution: We used a combination of methods, such as a drumstick with a piece of felt tightly bound to one end or a soft paintbrush which could be used as a pointer or an extension to the child's own arm. This served to ensure that, in spite of physical difficulties, children were still able to access the full range of opportunities provided by the interactive whiteboard.

Some children who did not have the physical skills required to reach with a pointer were encouraged where possible to use switch-adapted programs. The set-up menus of some programs allowed for children to touch any part of the screen in order to achieve a response.

The Soft Play Room is a safe environment in which children have developed their physical skills (alongside other skills such as communication and personal social and emotional skills). While doing so children have created and composed simple musical

Figure 7.2

pieces by moving up and down the soft stairs which act as a keyboard. Through the use of a wall-mounted pressure switch children have also influenced a series of lights in the cave/dark area.

Low-cost option: Similar learning outcomes could be achieved through the use of Musical Footprint toys, such as Funky Footprints and other music mats (See Appendix 1).

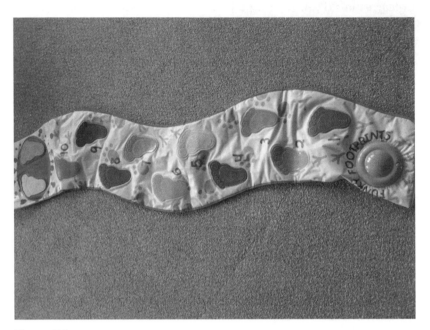

Figure 7.3

Children are able to influence the presence of visual effects when using the Hydrotherapy Pool. They can choose from combinations of UV lights, fibre-optic curtains and light projector, among others. They do this by using floating switches (the options available being pre-determined by the teacher).

We have a well-resourced Multi-Sensory Room where children can spend time operating a range of multi-sensory stimuli through the use of remote switches and pressure switches:

- fibre-optic lights
- bubble tubes
- projector and projector curtain
- tactile wall
- sound to light screen and switch-operated fan/wind machine.

Much of this equipment is open-ended; it can be used at an 'encounter' level where children are able to simply experience or be stimulated by the sensory output that the equipment provides. The equipment is also used to develop problem-solving skills; children are given 'remote switches' which operate specific equipment, and encouraged to operate a piece of equipment: for example, by pressing the switch they turn the bubble tube on or off. This activity can be developed to allow children to control two flat switches and hence two pieces of equipment. As a more challenging activity the practitioner could set up two switches, one to operate bubble tube A and the other to operate bubble tube B. Set both tubes onto a timer and allow children time with both tubes on. Then switch tube A or B off. Can they establish which switch operates which tube? Depending on the level of the child, the switches can be colour-coded, or have reference symbols or tactile objects attached to help make sense of the task.

Low-cost options: Much of the equipment in the Sensory Room is, by its very nature, very expensive. However, the motivating experiences can also be provided through the use of low-cost or budget equipment. The same activity as above can be carried out using switch-access toys. Another idea is:

- Use a very dark room or space. Add UV nail polish (available from most high-street fashion accessory shops) to pictures and use a UV torch. This is great for exploring counting and number rhymes. It really allows the children to focus on the number of elements in the number rhyme: for example, five fat sausages or five little firemen. The nail polish can either be applied to fingernails to represent the elements of the rhyme or applied to line drawings of the elements.

Likewise, fairgrounds, tourist attractions and seaside souvenir shops have provided ample opportunity to stock up on simple toys such as ducks that light up when put into water, or squashy balls that light up when you squeeze them, flash for a short period and then turn off without any action being taken. These are fascinating for the child who is simply 'encountering' or experiencing ICT, but equally magical for other Early Years children who can be challenged to consider how or why the light in the toy turns on and how it manages to turn itself off!

Acting as a motivator to many children

Working with a group of children with autism, we were keen to motivate the children to communicate and to help them gain an understanding of the purpose of communicating! We began by using some familiar communication devices before introducing some walkie-talkies.

The children were already familiar with using Big Macks and Talking Photo Albums: two pieces of low-tech equipment.

These low-tech pieces of equipment allow the user to record a short message (up to about 10 seconds) by simply pressing the small concealed 'Record' button at the same time as pressing the coloured 'plate' or 'disc' on the top of the aid.

The children were given plenty of opportunities to explore walkie-talkies. Having had lots of chances to press the buttons, hear the whistling noises and see the red light go on and off, we were ready to start sending messages!

Talking Photo Albums are another piece of low-tech equipment. Each page has a clear pocket for inserting a photograph (or any other picture) plus a small 'Play' button which allows a short message to be played back. (The message is recorded by simply pressing the 'Play' button and the 'Record' button simultaneously.)

I set up some Big Macks: each had a picture on the top and a recorded message such as 'Here is the fish.'

The Talking Photo Album had a series of pictures: one per page and a message about each picture recorded on the page.

Having set up the Big Macks and Talking Photo Albums and having had plenty of time for exploratory play, we were then ready for some structured activities.

Figure 7.4

Figure 7.5

The children took turns to sit on one side of a screen. They listened to a message through the walkie-talkie, e.g. 'Have you got the house?' Once they had located the picture of the house they could press the Big Mack and 'send' back the message using the walkie-talkie, for example, 'I've found the house!'

A similar structured activity was then carried out, using Talking Photo Albums instead of the Big Macks. After starting the activity in the same way, with the child behind the screen hearing a message such as 'Have you got the house?', the children

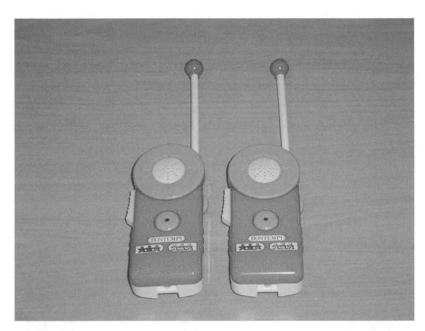

Figure 7.6

Figure 7.7 The children continued to use the walkie-talkie in their own play

were then encouraged to 'search' through a set of pictures in the Talking Photo Album and press the corresponding message.

The children were motivated to respond through using familiar and engaging equipment. The activity had a clear purpose, which helped to make the learning meaningful.

Linking real-life situations to learning

A group of children with autistic spectrum disorders were involved in designing and making a frozen yoghurt dessert. We wanted to involve the children as much as possible in the production of the dessert but were aware of the health and safety issues concerned with using food processors and blenders with sharp rotating blades!

We used a switch box to give the children access to the food processor and hand blender.

The switch box allows the practitioner to put distance between the child and the piece of equipment while still allowing them to have control over the equipment. The food processor is plugged into the switch box and the switch is also plugged into the switch box. By pressing the switch the child can operate the equipment safely.

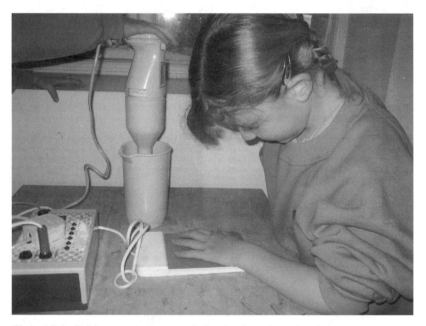

Figure 7.8 Children can be in control of technology through switch access

Making learning meaningful and relevant

Using PowerPoint to engage children with profound and multiple learning difficulties

In one class a child with profound and multiple learning difficulties had shown an interest in the interactive whiteboard and was occasionally motivated to walk over and touch the whiteboard. The class teacher wanted a simple program that would reward the child with a picture of her favourite characters each time she touched the screen. Initially we thought about developing a set of pages that I had prepared in Smart Notebook.

However, this was not successful, as her touches on the board were often fleeting or very short and she didn't have the persistence or hand strength to 'drag' a tree away from the teddy that was hiding behind it.

We felt that Microsoft PowerPoint might have the means to provide a series of

Figure 7.9

screens which, with the use of special 'transition' effects, could reveal a favourite character with a single touch anywhere on the screen.

After a relatively short time experimenting we came up with the basic template and have developed a series of PowerPoint slideshows with meaningful and motivating images. They are personal to individual children and can be used by and with the children to enhance adult-led experiences as well as being available for children's independent play and exploration. All it takes is a single touch on the screen and the slide moves on, revealing another motivating character or piece of music.

As part of a whole school 'World Cup Project', we created a series of slides with the England team theme song playing throughout the 'Slide Show'. Some of the older

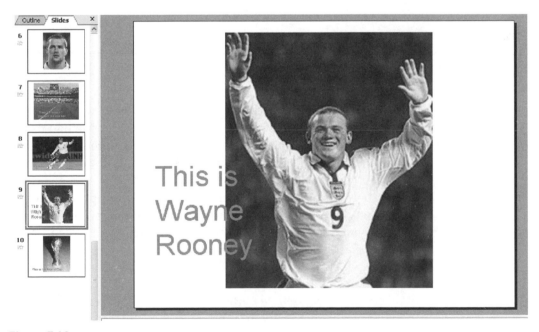

Figure 7.10

children were encouraged to suggest captions to go with each slide and some children were encouraged to read and record the captions. Thus we had a fully interactive and informative PowerPoint slideshow that could meet the wide-ranging needs of all the children in the class.

Easier but less personalised option: We also make good use of a fantastic website with a whole range of interactive slideshows that use popular and current trends in music and on TV to engage children in using the interactive whiteboard. See www.priorywoods.middlesbrough.sch.uk

Figure 7.11 ICT can encourage interaction

The Bookworm

This piece of equipment involves the recording of a book onto the memory card that is provided. As each page is recorded, it is necessary to attach a sticker to the page which aligns with one of the coloured (green or purple) membrane switches on the Bookworm. Although there are only eight membrane switches, it is possible to record longer books by using a sticky magnet (instructions are provided with the equipment).

We wanted to make the School Library a place where all children could share books regardless of their physical difficulties.

Once the book has been recorded it can then be re-read by simply touching a sticker which acts as a switch. It is also possible to plug an external switch pad into the Bookworm, thus enabling children who might find it difficult to press the small membrane switches to have access to the same book as their peers. As a school our next step is to look for ways in which we can develop 'tactile' switches on the pages so that some of the visually impaired children can gain further benefit.

Using the Bookworm allows children to participate with a degree of independence when 'reading' a book. It means that they can be active participants, enabling them to experience turn taking and to have control over the way in which the book is read.

Figure 7.12

Low-cost option: The Talking Book is costly and requires set-up time with the stickers and the recording before it can be used. For many children there are alternatives in the form of 'interactive' story books available in most bookshops that allow children to interact with the story through adding sound effects.

Allowing children to succeed (removing barriers to learning)

Clicker 5 is a program that enables children to create meaningful text through the use of grids and word banks, enhanced with pictures. The grids can be tailored to meet the individual needs and interests of children. They can be highly personalised as photographs and sound can be added to the grids. Clicker has enormous motivational potential as well as the obvious advantage that it can be altered to meet the needs of any session or almost any child.

Clicker offers us a particularly useful tool to support children with autism in our school. These children benefit from structure and knowing what is going to happen when and where, and Clicker works in a very structured way. Quite a lot of the success that our children experience with Clicker is due to the fact that their use of ICT is 'intuitive'. They may not necessarily be able to independently 'write a message that makes any sense' but they 'know which field the text should go in, how to move the cursor between fields and that you fill the field with symbols' and they can show this knowledge when they use Clicker (Guldberg 2002).

For example, Thomas worked out how to end the program by touching the 'home' icon and could open prepared grids, but he still had little understanding about the use of the grids for sentence making.

I looked at how the children coped with a familiar Clicker grid compared with their responses to a new grid. I found that there was little difference in the way that

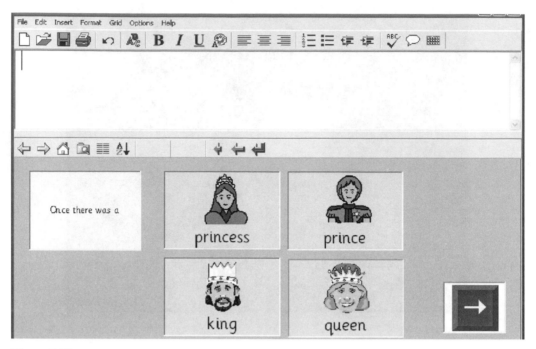

Figure 7.13

Rachel and Thomas reacted to the familiar and new grids, whereas George and Ellie were 'thrown' by the new grid. My observations led me to think that Rachel and Thomas had a much lower level of understanding of sentence building and saw the Clicker grid as objects to touch that then jumped to the top of the screen. George and Ellie, however, had understood that the grids were a means of combining text in a meaningful way. Because of this, George and Ellie had to process the new vocabulary in a grid and this slowed them down.

We have found that for children with autism in particular (but also for many children with other learning difficulties) the most successful activities are those which provide visual prompts and a 'scaffold' for them to work on. Clicker works on this premise, using a mixture of visual, auditory and kinaesthetic stimulation to encourage children to participate or engage in the learning activity.

Clicker is a generic tool for developing communication and literacy and has relevance to almost any area of learning within the Early Years curriculum and beyond.

Grids could be made to:

- record the daily weather;
- recount events of a trip or story;
- act as a stimulus in role play, bringing the home area, restaurant or shoe shop into the twenty-first century.

Use Clicker grids to prepare menus and select choices. Add your own photographs of resources used in the role play or from familiar 'real- world' environments.

There are many other ways in which the grids could be used. If text is needed for the activity, then a grid could be prepared to enable that text to be created!

Figure 7.14 ICT allows children to transfer skills

Low-cost option: Having 'thrown out' the old plastic pink kitchenette from the home corner, a group of children were encouraged to build their own using an old cardboard box and sticky paper and paint. Having built the new 'Multi-purpose kitchen island', we noticed that the quality of the children's play improved dramatically. The children had far greater ownership over their built kitchen. Making their own kitchen island gave children the opportunity to demonstrate the level of understanding they had of how the technology of a cooker works.

Not all ICT learning needs to use batteries and wires; there can be great value to be gained through encouraging children to create 'pretend technologies'. They can explore their own knowledge and understanding of technology as they build and have opportunities to talk with peers and adults about uses of technology.

Making pretend technologies:

- *Home role play*
  Making a television: how does it work, how can you change a channel, is there a remote control device?
- *Restaurant*
  Creating a microwave oven: does it have a plug, is there a pretend digital display, does it have any buttons to control the temperature and power?
- *Space centre*
  Making a computer for Mission Control: does it have a screen and a keyboard, are they connected through wires, has it got a plug to connect it to electricity?
- *Shop/garden centre*
  Making a bar code scanner or till: how will people pay, is there somewhere for them to swipe their debit card?

- *Vet/hospital*

   Making an x-ray machine: how will it work, where do the pictures come out, how will it be switched on and off?

A means of managing children's learning

Using a piece of ICT equipment such as Pixie has enabled children with limited communication skills to demonstrate their understanding of positional language and subsequently program Pixie independently.

We have 'dressed up' Pixie to act as a post office van or as Maisy's Bus, collecting all the passengers along a simple linear or grid route.

We also used Beebot to take part in a World Cup penalty shoot-out against Pixie! Some children were encouraged to program Beebot or Pixie to move straight towards the goal, while others were encouraged to take a corner and negotiate turns and suchlike in order to get the ball into the net!

Possibility of parental involvement

As a school we decided to carry out a survey into the children's uses of technology at home (see Appendix 4). We sent a questionnaire home to each child and their family. The results of the questionnaire were enlightening. They demonstrated that some children, who had significant needs, were engaging with quite complex technology and software in their homes. This was enlightening and led us to consider how we could best meet the needs of our pupils by ensuring that they were presented with equally challenging materials at school.

We also use ICT as a means for documenting and demonstrating the progress of children, using photographs and stills taken from video clips. In one instance, a child who was attending our 'Thursday Pre-School Group' demonstrated that he could move and co-ordinate both arms while using 'Keyboard Pounder' and was very motivated to do so (see www.littlebitsmultimedia.co.uk). We were able to take photographs and pass the information on to other agencies who were involved in drawing up programs for him, such as the physiotherapy team and the occupational therapists.

Photographic 'Learning Journeys' are now an established part of our termly evidence of children's learning, consisting of a series of photographs with a narrative commentary and learning objectives achieved, along with suggestions for the next steps in learning.

Conclusion

I have seen first hand the power that ICT has to motivate children and to help them make sense of the world around them by linking real-life situations to learning. ICT has the power to make learning meaningful and relevant, crossing the divide between work and play.

ICT equals empowerment to many children, as it allows them to make choices and interact with the world around them, where, without technology, they might not have the capability to make those choices.

8 ICT for practitioners

One 'star' is not enough

Sally Dennis

Teaching is a reflective and deeply human activity, an ethical enterprise that involves the teacher as a person.

(Coia and Taylor 2001)

Introduction

The Early Years workforce is not lacking the enthusiasm to develop children's learning through ICT. Rather, it is a workforce faced with challenges that affect the competence levels and therefore confidence levels of staff. Some settings have a clear vision and development plan for providing a broad-based and exciting approach to learning through ICT. Other settings can consist of staff who feel a sense of uncertainty about the potential of ICT, how to start, where to access training and support to ensure quality is at the heart of their provision.

All Early Years settings are unique in their structure and provision, and all are made up of staff who are committed to seeing children reach their educational potential. At the heart of education lies the educator ... and this chapter is designed with you in mind. It seeks to identify the significant role of each practitioner in the use of ICT in Early Years teaching and learning. The chapter is in three parts, looking at 'practitioner beliefs', 'practitioner competence' and 'practitioner confidence'.

If you are the 'ICT star' of your setting, then read this chapter with an open mind on how to develop the other staff in your team. If you see yourself as 'anything but the ICT star' of your team, then take heart and reflect on what might be holding you back from driving the use of ICT forward in your setting.

Due to the changing nature of technology this chapter is written in a principle-based format which can be generically applied to a setting with high and low levels of ICT resources and/or experience.

Practitioner beliefs

Before anything can be said about the confidence and competence of practitioners in the use of ICT, we must first reflect on the beliefs and understanding held by the practitioner, 'the person'. This section prompts reflection on our individual belief systems which underpin our motivation and openness to learning new ICT skills and, in turn, how we use these and collaborate with colleagues and children to develop our teaching practice.

Beliefs among Early Years educators vary and can include some staff embracing the possibilities of technology as a tool for learning and teaching, others embracing technology for its 'importance in society' and thus utilising it in the curriculum to ensure children have the necessary 'survival skills' for life, others, perhaps with reluctance, feeling obliged to use ICT, believing it is an imposed expectation within the curriculum.

It is common knowledge that what we believe affects the choices we make, and this is reflected in our behaviours, language and priorities. The important question to ask ourselves first is 'What do I believe about information and communications technology?'

My beliefs

What do I believe ICT is (and isn't)?

What do I believe about the role and value of ICT in society?

What do I believe about the role and value of ICT in my personal life?

What do I believe about the role and value of ICT for young children and technology?

What do I believe about the role and value of ICT in my teaching practice?

What does research tell me about the role and value of ICT for young children?

What does my experience tell me about the role and value of ICT for young children?

Each practitioner's thinking is unique, and therefore there are many views that can be held by staff. However, these examples serve to illustrate the link between beliefs and practice.

Example I

Having worked with young children for several years I am familiar with the core elements of what helps children to reach their educational potential. Without the use of ICT, children have been developing their emergent reading, writing and thinking skills through hands-on open-ended experiences. Now we have to make sure all children 'have a turn' on the computer because it is part of the Early Learning Goals within Knowledge and Understanding of the World. It is hard to have to fit it all in.

Practitioners who hold the belief that ICT is an imposed expectation are less likely to plan for and maximise the potential of ICT as a teaching and learning tool.

> **Example 2**
> In the early years of school, children are expected to use the computer for things such as their story making and mathematical development. In their early years we need to give children as many experiences of ICT as possible so that they are comfortable to learn through computers and various software programs when they start school. In the Early Years we encourage children to use the keyboard for learning letters and practising their name.

Practitioners who hold the belief that children must be given the opportunity to develop ICT skills for life are most likely to be skills focused in their use of ICT with children.

> **Example 3**
> A small group of children have been exploring mini beasts in our back garden. Last week we found a bug that we didn't know the name of. We collected it into a small dish and looked at it under the digital microscope, taking some stills for printing and a small video of the way it moved. Together we talked about how to find out more about the bug and agreed to look on the Internet for more information. The Internet has become like a library to us. We make the ICT work as a tool for us and the children learn and develop their 'ICT skills' in the process. After searching for images of the bug, I noticed that we could use images of different bugs to support children's skills understanding and language for 'same' and 'different'. Through this experience I realised I had always taught the children about a small number of mini beasts, only those that we had plastic replicas of, but now we are looking at so many types of bugs and mini beasts. The children are really interested in discovering, as it has come from their own interest. I have been thinking about the idea of making mini beast books and ways to create digital or printed stories from these.

Practitioners who use ICT for its possibilities are most likely to be creative and innovative in the way they plan for, introduce and develop learning through ICT. They are also more likely to explore and challenge the boundaries of a tool to discover its full potential. This is often a self-motivated approach which broadens experience and expertise in the process. Staff and children alike become learners of the ICT (developing ICT skills) in the process.

If we don't know what we believe about ICT it's often an indicator that we haven't 'engaged' with the purpose of using ICT and therefore it is less likely that we will be using ICT to its full potential. A good starting point is to look personally at the role of ICT in our own lives to start to understand its potential. Think about these situations:

> **The role of ICT in our personal life**
> Have you ordered a gift online for a friend?
>
> Do you buy your books from the high street or through online book stores?

Do you hire DVDs from your local video store or through the Internet?

Do you manage your bank accounts online?

Do you check your bank balance at a machine or with a bank teller each week?

Do you use the checkout at the grocery store that is self-service?

Do you text your family about when you are coming home?

Which technology experiences do I avoid?

Which technology experiences frustrate me?

Which technology experiences do I really appreciate?

Irrespective of the beliefs we may hold about the value added or deducted by technology, we are all using it to some degree within our daily lives. Have you ever found yourself, or heard your staff saying, 'I am not technological at all – I am not very good with computers'? It is easy to measure our expertise or 'lack of expertise' in ICT based on whether we think we 'know' much about the science of computers. This kind of belief can sabotage our confidence, and fails to take into consideration the large amount of ICT we competently and confidently use (sometimes unknowingly) in our day-to-day lives.

Expert or explorer?

Feeling inadequate about a subject can cause us to 'shy away' from the subject, or to delegate it to someone we consider more of an expert, in case we get it wrong. Some practitioners can see themselves as doing more 'harm' than good, or even fear the 'damage' they may cause to the technology due to their inexperience. This is evident in larger staff teams where several members will say, 'Oh, talk to Rebecca, she is a "whiz" with computers. She knows what she's talking about and we direct the children to her at the computer and for using the cameras.' The risk with this scenario is that Rebecca's skills continue to improve as she drives and delivers ICT experiences in the setting, but the remaining staff can continue to reinforce beliefs about themselves as incompetent and unconfident for the role. Delegating or diverting responsibility for ICT can also leave the staff team without opportunities to progress their own skills and understanding. The dynamic can often represent a belief that ICT is an 'add-on to the curriculum' where a specialist can 'cover' that subject, but with all other subjects or areas of learning all staff must take full ownership to value and teach in each area. I am in no way suggesting that Early Years settings don't need an ICT co-ordinator', rather I want to challenge the sometimes confused notion of 'co-ordinator'.

Delegating or diverting responsibility for ICT can limit the experiences of children, who are restricted to learning and using ICT only with the 'expert' staff member. The 'expert's' time is also diluted across the whole group and it is less likely that they can pick up on the individual initiatives and ideas of children while learning and exploration is in action.

Frequently, many competent users would still define themselves as 'not very technological'. This self-perception is usually due to knowing that others know more than they do and/or because they cannot explain why the technology works the way it does. Putting this into perspective, ICT is a vast and complex subject and no single individual can 'know everything' about ICT. Even those who could be considered specialists in ICT are not necessarily in a better position than Early Years practitioners because they may not know how to make the connection between ICT possibilities and the understanding and engagement of a young child. It's important that we use our expertise with children, to drive and inform our decision making on new and innovative ways for children to learn about and through ICT.

Can you spot the 'star'?

Scenario: 'ICT for a purpose'

Nisha and I wanted to give the children an experience of seeing themselves as part of a story through the use of a video camera. We don't have a special video camera like some centres, so we decided to use the video feature on the digital camera that we use in the classroom.

Nisha and I hadn't used the video feature on the digital camera before so we decided to combine our activities to learn together. Nisha was introducing the big story 'Handa's Surprise' to her group, and I was focusing on counting, using the fruits from the story. We agreed to make a story together that could be the video. I was going to use the camera and Nisha was going to introduce the story and then get the children to act it out using the plastic fruits I had for counting. We told the children that we were going to make a video of the story, and that first we needed to learn how to use the video on the camera. I underestimated the number of things we could learn from this experience. Here are some of the learning experiences we covered.

Discussion
(making links to familiar experiences and prior learning)

Nisha told the children that we didn't know how to use the video feature on the camera and asked the children if any of them had made a video before. The children began to talk about videos and video machines and 'Daddy's movie' from the holiday. The discussion highlighted that the children were familiar with being filmed and that if we really got stuck we could draw on the skills of the parents. Two of the children started to talk about their video players and the discussion led to favourite movies.

Problem solving
(collaborating on ideas and solutions)

I asked the children to help me with getting started: 'What do you think I should do first?' 'Press the buttons,' said one child. I tried to, but nothing changed. I told the children and asked what I should do. 'Turn it on,' said another. 'Batteries

---

broken,' said another. The children were very familiar with using the cameras themselves as we have taught them about using digital photography. One child came to help me switch it on.

The teacher the learner

Using the icons on the menu dial I fixed the camera to the 'video' symbol simply through a process of elimination. Together we tested to see if we could take a short film. This was really straightforward but I hadn't estimated that the filming would cut out after two minutes. After viewing and deleting a few of the samples with the children, we decided to get started. Nisha and I didn't know how to change how long a video could last so we decided to deliver and record our story in short chunks. It's funny because I hadn't realised that it was easier to make short little clips rather than try to get it all in order as one long film.

Reviewing through ICT
(reviewing my own learning and the learning of others)

Nisha began with the story first and read it in full, and some children joined in the activity along the way. She then explained to the children that we were going to make a 'Handa's Surprise' film for the nursery and that we would use dress-ups, baskets and fruits for counting. Nisha selected five children to be 'Handa' and gave them a basket to balance on their head. Five other children were selected to be 'Akeyo' and they waited on the other side of the room for Handa to arrive. At the count of three, the children being Handa had to walk to Akeyo balancing the basket without using their hands. There was so much laughter as baskets fell and hands went up to hold them.

It was quite a focused task for the individual children and they didn't get to watch the other children because the experience took so much concentration. We decided to film this experience so that the children could watch themselves and also each other. The children's engagement surprised me, and they were almost pushing to see the screen. I noticed that they seemed to enjoy seeing themselves in the film more than balancing the basket. I was really frustrated with trying to show the small screen back to all the children, so I remembered something that Bindu had shown me from the photos, and I plugged the camera into the TV so we could watch the replays on a larger screen. I started to introduce the counting, by asking the children to review the video and watch how many steps 'Peter' took before he dropped the basket. Some children found it difficult to count the steps of only one child among many, so we decided to remake the films involving one child at a time. We then played back the video and counted the steps together. It was really useful to be able to rewind and count again.

Planning together

Nisha commented on the time; we had been having so much fun I hadn't realised that we had used all of the time we had. We hadn't even begun the learning experiences we had planned for but I was enlightened by all that had come from the experience of getting started. We asked the children whether they would like to help with the Handa story tomorrow. Nisha asked the children how we could make the story ourselves and put it on to the video. She facilitated the discussion by asking about what things Handa needed in her basket and who else needed to be in the story. They made a list out of children's drawings of the items. This helped us to think about the kinds of things to bring to the next day's activity. It was also a good way to review the story and create a calm end to the experience. We asked the children to sit down again while Nisha silently showed the pictures of the story without using words.

Reflecting as a team

The children had been so excited to participate in the basket walk and to see each other on the screen, it had been quite a noisy session. Excess noise makes the filming difficult, so I wasn't sure how to improve the recording. At the end of the day Nisha and I agreed to talk with the children about the best way to manage sound levels for recording. We didn't want to stifle the children's enthusiasm by constantly asking them to be quiet or by formalising the re-enactment so much that children became shy. We wondered if asking the children about the noise levels and being able to play back examples might help them to understand they have a part to play in making the film work. I wondered, too, if playing back the film without the picture would help them to tune into their own voice and the voice of others. Perhaps that is another activity in itself.

Nisha and I decided that we would join up again for a joint session the following day and start the session by practising different sound levels and voice levels with the children and listening back to these on the camera.

I was becoming a bit concerned that what I had originally planned had not been achieved and I wanted the IT to enhance the experience, not hijack it. Nisha and I agreed to build on the day's learning and make it a two-day experience using the camera again the next day. I told the rest of the staff about how the activity went and Sarah said it was probably a good thing that we didn't start with the counting and camera at the same time, because the children were primarily focused on seeing themselves, and would probably be more receptive on the second day to counting as a focus.

Nisha said she would have a look on the Internet to find out about how long you can make a film for on the camera. Mandy said she still had the box and manual for the camera in the resource cupboard and that it might explain how to change the settings. I said I would search the resource cupboard for the microphone we used to use, as this might help to give better quality of sound for the storytellers tomorrow.

We realised that giving the children visual and audio feedback of themselves was very interesting and important to them. Rachel asked if she could use the camera on Friday as she wanted to continue the basket balancing activity outside, using her obstacle course, and thought that maybe children could do the course in pairs, one filming the other one who is balancing the basket, to mirror today's activity. I suggested that the filming might be too hard for the children but that they could start with stills and use video with some support. Nisha pointed out that I might be underestimating the children, as the only real difference from what they can already do with the cameras was in getting the camera set to the right function (video) and then holding the button down to film. It made me think about how the children might be able to develop their own balance while filming (just like those with a basket), as they have to walk and aim the camera at the same time.

In this example the children have hands-on experience of the journey of learning about and through ICT. The 'star' of the scenario 'ICT for a purpose' is not identifiable; rather, all members of the team are contributing and learning even to the point of collaborating on ideas. The staff were not experts but they decided to team up to help each other, and best of all they invited the children to think about and contribute to the learning process. The children's ideas were welcomed and valued through the discussion and the sense of fun for both staff and children made them lose track of time. The learning that was planned was not achieved in the timeframe they anticipated, but the activities opened up a greater understanding of the children's prior experiences with ICT and highlighted experiences and technologies that motivate them. It also gave the children a good foundation for becoming familiar with the equipment before getting started with film and story making on the second day. The activity also highlighted to the staff that the children had a lot to offer and that many learning experiences could be developed through using the cameras.

The breadth of ownership of ICT among the team meant that they were committed to:

- using an ICT tool without being an expert;
- helping and supporting each other as learners;
- modelling themselves as learners to the children;
- learning from and about the children's knowledge and experience of ICT;
- finding solutions without depending on a specialist;
- building on each other's ideas and use of ICT;
- making use of the ICT resources they have.

When the whole staff team share ownership of the use of ICT, the development of children's ICT competencies and initiatives can take place throughout all the children's experiences in the setting.

Self-check

Do I have to know how to use the equipment well before I can use it with the children?

Does it matter if I don't get it right the first time?

When did I last collaborate to help and support another team member in using ICT?

When did I last model being a learner with the children?

What do I know about the children's knowledge and experience of ICT?

What do I know about their home experiences of ICT and the potential of involving parents in using ICT in the setting?

When did I last identify something new that I want to learn about technology?

When did I last offer to help build on my colleagues' ideas and use of ICT?

Am I aware of what resources we have? Have I used all or most of these resources within my teaching?

An alternative to the experience in the scenario 'ICT for a purpose' could have been that video making be left to the 'ICT expert' of the team. Nisha could have read her big book independently and invited the children to re-enact the story first with balancing baskets and then moving into the sequence of collecting and transporting the fruits for Akeyo (the partner). Without the video tool to replay, the children would not have been able to review their own actions and watch their peers.

Without the discussion with the children, the staff might not have discovered which children had had experiences with filming and using cameras in the home and with their family. The ICT expert could have introduced the film making, but without the link to the story which had helped the children to engage and get into character. This risk of leaving all the ICT teaching to the 'expert' means that person can become entirely 'ICT skills'-focused and lose the value of establishing a meaningful context and purpose for using ICT in children's learning.

Without attempting the video activity, the staff would have been unlikely to have explored the Internet for answers, searched the resource cupboard to find the microphones, and made links between the story and outside play. As educators we understand that exploration extends children's thinking and knowledge, and that the challenges rest in valuing this process for ourselves in the use of ICT.

The detailed scenario highlights the need to share ownership and skill development in ICT, not as a specialism for one 'star' but as a core element to all teaching practice. Shared ownership and skills in ICT widens the opportunity to embed ICT across the curriculum and widens the opportunity for children to learn about and through ICT in meaningful ways.

Sharing the vision

How can a team share and embrace a vision if they don't know what each person believes and is committed to? It's also difficult to share a vision for ICT in the setting if the beliefs of individuals within the team are not aligned or understood. Sharing our beliefs can help us to understand each other more, and gives an opportunity to invite and support professional development. Knowledge of each other's beliefs can also strengthen and support team dynamics, and therefore drive the quality of teaching practice in a collaborative way that consistently promotes both individual and team reflection and self-improvement.

In the context of settings where there are more than two staff working together, there can be an inconsistent message on care and commitment to ICT in practice. Simply because there is an 'expert' who is considered to have responsibility for ICT, they can easily become the 'only person' responsible for ICT. In the case where there are two members of staff in the centre/class, the beliefs of one staff person can dominate the innovative use or lack of use in ICT, because in simple terms they make up 50 per cent of the team. Either way, each individual (no matter the size of the staff group they work in) has an important part to play and each individual's thinking has an influence on the overall teaching practice of the centre.

How much do you know about what your colleagues believe about ICT? As a team, take time to reflect and explore each other's beliefs about ICT.

Our beliefs

What do you believe ICT is (and isn't)?

What do you believe about the role and value of ICT in society?

What do you believe about the role and value of ICT in your personal life?

What do you believe about the role and value of ICT for young children and technology?

What do you believe about the role and value of ICT in your teaching practice?

What does research tell you about the role and value of ICT for young children?

What does your experience tell you about the role and value of ICT for young children?

Do you believe your setting has high-quality ICT provision for children?

Quietly holding individual differences in beliefs can be the barriers to working together with synergy and innovation, not because the beliefs are different but because the beliefs are not understood. When you have asked the above questions of your colleagues, consider looking at how these views can be integrated to strengthen the settings vision for ICT. This process can draw out the strength of individuals in the team and trigger discussion about peer support for those staff who are willing and/or wanting to develop their use of ICT in their practice.

If you are in a team where the value placed on ICT is inconsistent and in some aspects nonexistent, asking the above questions may help to resolve *why* this is the case. The set of questions give you an objective tool to facilitate honesty, and dialogue that challenges and stimulates thinking, reflection and personal ownership.

Preparing to ask the questions

Who is the best person or group of people to be asking the questions among the team?

What is the best forum for asking these questions?
Do staff know why they are being asked questions?

What boundaries need to be established in order to facilitate honest and reflective responses?

Practitioner competence

ICT skills and understanding go hand in hand. When we understand the breadth of what makes up ICT, we can begin to explore and link together the potential of ICT as a learning and teaching tool.

Understanding

What do I understand ICT to be?

What ICT do children encounter in their daily lives?

What can children learn about ICT?

What can children learn through the use of ICT?

What ICT resources do we have in the setting?

Am I competent in using each of these?

How and where can I develop my own ICT skills?

What resources are available to me to develop my own skills?

What external examples of expertise and/or aspiration can be used for developing my competence and that of the whole team?

It is important to understand that as a practitioner you don't need to know everything before you can use ICT, nor is it possible to know everything about ICT as it is undergoing constant change and development. Knowing why you are using ICT is critical to effective application. This is true of any program, tool or application that you might choose to use in your setting, and gives meaning to your own learning as you discern the purpose and suitability of what you will use and where and when it can be used.

The scenario 'ICT for a purpose' which involved making stories with the video cameras is a good example of exploration at its best. It is appropriate to say, however, that the practitioners in this scenario had been using ICT in the classroom for some time. They had a foundation of knowledge and experience to be experimental with the tools and to learn with the children.

Table 8.1 outlines a range of tools and how they can be used in practice. Importantly, the table identifies the types of questions and reflections that a practitioner can apply when using or planning to use these tools. High-quality ICT provision does not require settings to have all of these resources, nor is the list exhaustive. It is simply a list of tools that can be used in multiple ways and in this case the focus is on using the tools in your documentation of children's learning. These same tools can be powerful resources in the hands of children.

Table 8.1

ICT tool	Practitioner thinking	Practice
(A) Collecting data Digital camera	• What images do I want to take and for what purpose? • Can children, staff and parents use the camera? • Have I/we encouraged self-initiated use of the camera? • Does everyone know where to find and return the camera to? • What makes an effective photograph? Is it the resolution, the subject matter, the spontaneity, the genuine encounter uninterrupted by the presence of a camera? There is no right or wrong answer to this question but it is something to explore as an individual and as a whole team, giving thought to the purpose of the image.	• Learning to use the camera is best achieved through hands-on exploration. • Have the camera nearby. • Rechargeable batteries can be ready each day by using a duplicate rotation. • Keep downloading regularly among staff so that you can always start with a clean/empty memory card. • Utilize zoom to capture the detail and sequences of learning experiences. • Help each other as a team by photographing each other's engagement with children (reducing disruptions to the flow of an experience).
Digital video	• Why video and not stills? • Do I need to use a digital video camera or can I simply use the video feature on the standard digital camera? • What is the audio in the area like? • What will be the best angle to capture in this experience? • How discreet do I want the presence of the camera to be? • Am I prepared to take the time to review the footage? • What documentation do I need to capture parallel to the digital video? • Do I have a thread of focus to the review or is it open-ended? • How can I increase my skills in the digital video processes?	• Be aware of your own voice and the voices of those you are capturing. • Use tripods where possible. • Look for opportunities to involve parents and children in the video process. • Plan your video review beforehand and assign roles to the team if there are special focus threads. • Use timing in your notes when documenting to make any returns to the footage as efficient as possible.
Scanner	• Is the scanner accessible to children and adults alike? • Does the set-up enable self-initiated use? • How skilled are our staff and children in scanning to print? • How skilled are our staff and children in knowing where to save and edit scanned images?	• Wherever possible save scanned images as picture files, not directly into a document. This allows you to use it as a master file to use across multiple files and it can easily be located again. Images scanned directly into files mean that they can only be specifically found within that file, and would need to be copied and then pasted into other documents. • Picture files e.g. jpg/bmp files, can also be used in slideshows without ever being inserted into other documents.
(B) Organising data PC/laptop	• What are the staff skill levels in the use of the PC? • Do we promote opportunity to share, practise and develop skills? • How is confidence in the use of the computer developed?	• Windows XP provides a very visual and generic means of managing digital images and devices. Slideshows can be viewed, images renamed, rotated and regrouped with simplicity.

Category	Questions	Notes
	• What training can we access to develop both our understanding and skill development? • How are we promoting peer training and development among staff? • How accessible is the PC/laptop for adults, children and parents? • At what point do we need to upgrade our PC/laptop?	• Win XP includes the FREE feature of the 'Camera and Scanner Wizard', which enables the use of any brand of camera or card reader by using the same USB port and the same step-by-step process. This can effectively reduce training and streamline the skill requirements of staff who are using multiple types of cameras and equipment.
User access	• Who has 'access' to the PC in our setting? • Who do we see as co-constructors of the documentation process? • How supportive is our set-up to the type of user?	• Win XP allows the set-up of different users on the computer. Keeping the storage of staff files separate from children's files allows children to explore and manage their own folders/files without the risk of losing months of staff records. • Involving children in the process of set-up, navigation and shutdown helps to develop their ICT literacy, and the use of visual icons for programs and folders can mean that children can navigate with confidence without having to have a high level of reading skills. • Exposure and support in developing visual literacy skills can challenge our expectations/assumptions of children's abilities.
File management	• Do all staff have a clear understanding of where to create, save, rename and relocate files? • Have we made file management a priority and feature of our entire PC-based ICT training? • Have we identified files to share as a team and files to manage as individuals? • Have we planned and implemented a regular back-up system to ensure that all data is secure?	• Plan as a team how you would like to organise your files, e.g. some settings organise the created files into individually named staff folders and children's folders. The digital imaging files (stills, video and scanned files) are then stored in a shared space so that they can be accessed by all of the staff team. • File naming is crucial to making file management efficient. Win XP allows the user to rename a batch of images when downloading, and also allows the user to rename a single file or group of files with ease. • Keep in mind that files have their own download date, so naming a file by date is not needed, nor is it useful for referencing. Think about whether the names of the people in the photo or the type of experience captured is going to be most useful. • If you want to locate the date of a file it can be viewed in the 'details' view within the window or simply right-click the file and select 'properties'.
Programs	• What program will give me the most options in sharing the data? • How can I streamline the amount of training required for all of the programs that we have available? • How am I going to make the most of the digital capacity of the files I have created? • Have I taken time to explore and understand the capacity of the program? • What extra steps can I take to extend my skills each time I use the program?	• To streamline the amount of training required and the number of processes to remember, try wherever possible to use the one program for several purposes, e.g. Microsoft PowerPoint is designed to integrate text and images/media. It allows you to rearrange content easily, to view slideshows and to print in multiple types of formats. It can be used in a portrait or landscape layout and includes the drawing and picture toolbar features in the same way as MS Word. (reference to simple training skill module http://www.seyec.com/web/00_ict_resources_01.html for the Drawing and Picture Tool Bar).

Table 8.1 – *Continued*

ICT tool	Practitioner thinking	Practice
(C) Sharing data Printer	• Do I really need to print? • Who am I printing for and to what size? • Have we planned to make printing a possibility for adults and children alike? • The question of photo paper versus plain paper and black and white versus colour can only be answered by the setting. Plain paper absorbs more ink than glossy paper and this then needs to be contrasted with the cost of photo paper over plain. • The most important thing is to be very clear about the purpose of printing, to know the audience and context intended for sharing and engaging others in the documentation.	• Is the printer accessible and ready for the adult or child to use instantly? • Is a selection of paper types provided and easily at hand? • Is the printer at child height and able to be used without disrupting any other learning experiences taking place around it? • Have we thought about A4 and A3 printing?
Storage and back-ups	• Clear file management makes the storage of content and back-up content very simple. With a shared team approach, the staff know what, where and how to find files and can identify dates and details as required.	• Back-up copies of data should be regular and treated as confidential. The type of storage can range from CD-ROM/S to memory pens, external hard drives, other PCs or servers. School-based settings may already have guidelines and systems in place that utilise the school network. • Wherever possible save onto the one device or location. Individual floppy disks, CD-ROMs, etc. can become more confusing than helpful. • A simple way to start the new year and to ease the amount of digital imagery to scroll through is to move all folders into a 'History' folder and create new sets of folders for the new year. There is always an overlap between ideas and timing and this allows efficient use of the regular files and easy access to previous work, which may be relevant to a project or document you are working on.
Sharing data	• Who do I want to see these files? • How will they best be shared? • How will I capture the response and developments that extend from sharing the documentation? • Am I providing opportunities for adults and children to access and add to the digital documentation?	• Data can be shared in printed formats such as books, wall displays, 3-D displays, in and on the surface of objects and furniture. • Data can also be shared in a digital format by viewing files, slideshows through PCs, TVs and interactive whiteboards. • Data can be shared across or between computers via floppy disks, CDs, memory sticks, compact flash cards, across a network, and online.

Data protection is an important element to consider in our Early Years' practice. The use of images and video footage for external sources and websites must have the full written approval of parents and, wherever possible, names and images should not be displayed together. It is best to seek the advice of your local authority or governing organisation to ensure you are aware of your data protection obligations. Incorporating a simple photo release approval statement on to your registration form can save administration time and allows you to keep a bank of names of children whose image must not be used externally. An example of such a form is given in Appendix 11.

These examples are not conclusive, nor are they meant to be prescriptive; they are simply examples of the way some Early Years centres have developed their ICT.

Practitioner confidence

Our confidence levels are directly affected by:

- the way we see ourselves;
- the way we perceive others to see us;
- our experiences of success or failure;
- what we expect of ourselves;
- the potential others see and expect in us.

Learning to learn

How we see ourselves as learners has a direct impact on the learning process itself. Internal messages to ourselves or external announcements to peers that we are 'not technological' only reduce our expectations of ourselves and set us up with an expectation to fail or render us inadequate for the task. How we see ourselves and what we say about ourselves is powerful and can fuel or dilute our self-doubt.

The important thing to focus on is the purpose of our learning. If we are learning something for a specific purpose, we will more easily be able to test and apply it in context and this will enhance our learning and gives us opportunities to practise and develop our skills.

Seeing ourselves as learners rather than experts can help to take the pressure off, and allows all practitioners to develop from the point they have reached in their skills and experience. Sharing the attitude of 'being a learner' will provide a safe and encouraging climate in the staffroom and in planning meetings to share successes and challenges in using ICT.

In many cases staff apply a climate of 'permission to explore' for children but do not apply this principle to themselves or their peers. It's important to take hold of our own thinking and encourage ourselves as learners through professional development opportunities such as training. We also need to provide ourselves with practical opportunities to practise our learning and, importantly, with the internal encouragement to take risks and extend our understanding and experience even if it doesn't all go quite to plan. Equally we can encourage each other through peer teaching, joint planning, discussion and feedback. A climate where all staff and children are co-learners will help to invite the scaffolding of ideas and the strengthening of skills sets among the team.

Practically speaking

As a team, agree to sayings that are encouraging and solution focused. Creating this list as a team can help to identify existing self-doubt in the team, and provide permission to encourage each other towards positive expectations of one's self and each other.

Some examples are given in Table 8.2.

Table 8.2

Self-doubt	Solution-focused alternative
I can't take quality photos, they are blurry all the time.	Some of my photos work well, others are blurry, which can be frustrating. I am going to allow myself five minutes this morning to practise the quality of my photos.
I wish I wasn't based at the computer station this morning; something always goes wrong.	Today I am not going to panic when something doesn't work at the computer station. I am going to start a log book of problems and talk to Rebecca at the end of the session to see where things might be going wrong.
I don't know much about the digital microscope; it is probably better if Rebecca does the activity, not me.	The activity could work well using the digital microscope. I don't know much about how it works, so we are going to postpone the activity by one day so that I can peer-teach with Rebecca or Iram, who can show me how to use the microscope while we use it with the children.

It is easy to fall into the trap of 'educators must have all of the answers', when educators are equally learners in the changing world of technology. Among your parent community, there are, no doubt, mixed levels of competence and indeed of confidence in the use of ICT, for parents who are users of ICT in their personal and professional lives. Even those parents who are perhaps leading in the field of ICT in their workplace can have uncertainties and require new knowledge to stay abreast of changes in the industry. When a staff team is comfortable with the perspective of being 'learners', knowledge and expertise can be brought in from a range of sources including the parent community. In some cases the need for support and help with ICT can be a useful means of inviting and increasing parental involvement in the nursery.

> Parental involvement programmes should be geared in the direction that best meets the needs of the students, parents and immediate community.
>
> (Bermudez *et al.* 1992)

Start with something

It's never too late to start learning about ICT and how it can be used in a powerful way to support young children's learning and to improve teaching practice. Important to this process is the honest reflection on the beliefs that we hold about ICT and its role and value in our personal and professional lives and the lives of the young children we work with.

What is one belief you hold and can challenge?

Competence has to start somewhere, even if this means starting with 'nothing' and building to 'something'. The journey needs to begin so that you can become a successful and effective user of ICT within your teaching practice.

What is one area in which you can develop your competence?

Confidence is hinged on the success of our experience with ICT and is closely linked to beliefs about ourselves and the perceptions of others.

What is one saying you say to yourself or others about your ICT competence that can be challenged?

9 Parents as partners*

Harriet Price

Introduction

Many chapters of this book have raised the importance of working with parents. By working with families in developing skills and knowledge in using technology, we can:

- understand children's home experiences of technology;
- support families in their uses of technology with their children and build a common understanding of the role technology in our lives;
- use technology to involve parents further in their children's development and achievements.

Understand children's home experiences of technology

Children grow up in technologically rich environments.

They have been called our digital natives (Prensky 2001). They are born into worlds rich in technology. By understanding this we can begin to build up a picture of the experiences they bring with them to a setting and work better in partnership with parents and carers to help children gain a sense of mastery over the technology around them and to empower them with its many uses for learning.

Technology is an integral part of all our lives; in our homes we have remote controls for television sets and video recorders, toys that have buttons and buzzers, phones and mobile phones, washing machines, microwaves and other machines that require programming.

Outside the home children are also immersed in our technological world; they see automatic doors, cash machines, barcode scanners, digital tills and weighing machines, security cameras – the list can go on and on. Technology is part of children's everyday lives and our settings need to reflect a familiar environment for children to develop a sense of belonging and to be able to play with and experience tools that have cultural significance.

---

* This chapter is based on work at Homerton Children's Centre, Cambridge.

Children are naturally curious and they will explore not only how technology works but also how it fits into the world they live in. Research carried out through Stirling University, 'Already at a disadvantage?' (McPake *et al.* 2005), found that practitioners rarely consider children's developing ICT cultural and learning competences and give greater emphasis to children's technical competencies.

In other words, we are paying too much attention to ICT skills, e.g. can children use a mouse, can they click and drag? And not enough attention to technology used for learning, e.g. how can I plan for a child to use a digital camera to communicate things they have done, or how can I support children in writing labels for our setting? Perhaps too little attention is paid to cultural competence; do we offer enough opportunities for children to explore, play with and talk about the large range of technologies they come across in their homes?

We need to make ourselves aware of children's home experiences with technology so that we can build on what they know and can do. To help us build a picture of the experiences children bring with them we can:

- Invite families to tell us about their child's interests, e.g. perhaps on a home visit or initial visit to the setting, through informal conversation or by offering a context such as making an 'all about me' book together.
- Observe children at play using a range of technology. Observations can show us children's home experiences with technology. For examples of observations of children using ICT, and summaries of what this can tell us about children's previous experiences, see 'Observations of children at play with ICT' on the website: Foundation.e2bn.org
- Talk with parents on a regular basis, inviting two-way communication on their child's interests, learning and development.
- Listen to parents' stories about their children's experiences of technology at home.
- Build 'cardboard box' technology with children (TV, computer, DVD player, microwave, etc.) and have open discussion with children about what these are and what we do with them. This will help build a picture of what children know about technology.

Support families in their uses of technology with their children and build a common understanding of the role of technology in our lives

Parents and carers will have many varying opinions about what technology is and what it might offer their children. Many families may think that if we talk about the children's experiences of technology we are only referring to computers. It is up to practitioners to open up a dialogue about what technology is in young children's lives and why it is important to them. Some families might be concerned about children's uses of some technologies; for example, they may think it is not appropriate for a three-year-old to access a computer. By involving parents in what we are doing and why, we may alleviate some fears and support them in making choices about what they provide at home. Equally, by listening carefully, we can learn how to complement children's home experiences. For example, we find many children at Homerton are used to playing on CBeebies in their homes. We often use this program to help children 'settle in'; it's familiar to them and straight away they find they have some common ground with other children. However, knowing they can continue to access this at home, we move the children on to more open-ended software that challenges their creativity and leads them to thinking a little further. We involve parents and children in using this software together. A computer with our software is set up in the reception area for children, parents and carers to use at any time) and they are able to purchase this software through the catalogues we provide (see Appendix 1, Software and resources; many publishing companies offer reduced prices on software for home use).

We can help support families in their uses of technology with children through:

- encouraging conversation with parents about the child's use of ICT in the home setting;
- communicating with families about their child's skills, knowledge and understanding about technology;
- giving information about suitable resources: hardware, software and ICT toys;
- recognising parents' possible anxieties and responding appropriately, so that if they are concerned about their child's use of a computer, help them with information about appropriate software and showing how to manage computer times so that it is balanced with other play;
- by acting as models, using technology well ourselves; using technology to communicate with parents through, for example, email, websites, newsletters, digital photographs, large monitors/screens to display information.;
- making available books and leaflets on ICT for parents to browse or borrow (see box below);
- ensuring parents are involved in our ICT policy remembering to get their written permission for using photographs of their children;
- putting on courses or workshops around specific themes, e.g. using a computer with young children, or everyday technology and children's play, or children's use of the Internet;
- using www.myguide.co.uk to offer online courses for parents and carers to improve their own computer and Internet skills.

A booklist to start a 'library' for parents and carers

More than Computers: Information and Communications Technology in the Early Years by Iram Siraj-Blatchford and John Siraj-Blatchford.

- This book identifies principles of good practice for developmentally appropriate ICT for children. It explores why it is important for children to be confident users of ICT. It identifies how practitioners and parents can support children's development in this area, and looks at the issues that should be considered for a healthy, balanced approach to this aspect of our modern world. Available from Early Education, www.early-education.org.uk

Supporting Information and Communications Technology in the Early Years by John Siraj-Blatchford and David Whitebread.

- This book helps readers to understand how very young children (from birth to six) develop an early awareness of technologies and subsequently develop their knowledge, skills and understanding of Information and Communications Technology.

The Little Book of ICT by Andrew Trythall.

- In the popular 'Little book' series. Full of activities, including the use of computer paint programs, music making and movie making, using ICT in role play, dance and visits. The breadth will encourage children's learning in all areas of development. Available from Featherstone Education, www.featherstone.uk.com

Belair Early Years: Hands on ICT by Graham Parton.

- This book is full of colour photographs and good ideas for teaching ICT in the early years. It has been designed to build confidence and will be of interest to practitioners and parents alike. There is a home-links section for children to develop activities at home.

Early Education: Young Children and Technology.

- As part of the 'Learning Together' series, Early Education have produced a leaflet on young children and technology for parents and practitioners. This can be downloaded from www.early-education.org.uk

We can use technology to communicate with families in a number of ways:

- With the Internet translate common words into other languages, so you are able to use them with children and their families, e.g. you could make your own 'Welcome' poster. There are many examples on the Internet with 'Welcome' or 'Hello' translated into many languages.
- Use photographs in your talks with families about their children's progress to support what you are saying. Use slideshows of photographs through a digital photo frame or plasma screen at the end of sessions to show families what their children have been doing.
- Make a 'special book' of photos that celebrates children's interests and achievements. Children could contribute to this with their families as well as the setting.
- If possible, build a website (get in touch with your local authority to see how they can help and what they provide) to involve families in the setting, particularly those parents who work long hours and find it hard to attend.
- If possible, offer to be in touch with families through email or/and text messaging. ICT can help to maintain our regular contact with families.
- Use digital video to share our observations of children's learning with parents.

Use technology to involve parents further in their children's development and achievements

Case study

We share children's ongoing achievements with families through 'special books' (which are built up over the time children are at Homerton). Children take ownership over their books, adding photographs, pictures and printouts that are important to them, and they can take their books home and add to them with their families. We have also begun using a Virtual Learning Environment (VLE) to share children's learning, play, interests and achievements between home and setting.

A VLE is a web-based online environment that includes tools for adding content. VLEs are used to support the teaching and learning processes through delivering content online. At Homerton Children's Centre we are working with a VLE developed in Cambridgeshire called Starz. We are using Starz to share children's learning with families through two-way communication. A child is able, with practitioner support, to add photographs, videos, audio or files (perhaps a scanned image of a painting) to their own secure space within Starz. At home they can share this with their families and, more powerfully, their families can support them in adding photographs, videos, audio or files of their play, interests and learning at home. With the help of practitioners or their families, children can add comments to the site, allowing two-way communication between home and setting.

The implications of this are powerful. Families who find it hard to visit the setting can become more involved in sharing their children's learning and development. Families are able to have a greater voice in how they see their own children developing; by contributing to a website, they can reflect home life more fully. Photos of an outing to a park, how they have celebrated their child's birthday, a grand-dad coming to visit, can all be shared on a regular basis with the setting. Children are at the heart of this communication, and we emphasise to families that this is about the 'child's voice'. Just as they take ownership of their 'special books', their own space in Starz is their unique record of things they like to do, things they are interested in, their achievements and pleasures. By building up their own gallery of photos, video, comments and so on, they come to see themselves as learners and achievers.

There are difficult issues surrounding the introduction of a VLE into Early Years, not all of which we have been able to resolve. These are some of the challenges we have, and continue, to meet!

- Not all children will be interested enough in technology to enjoy sharing their learning with their families. This causes some practitioners concern over equality of provision.
- Not all families will be interested in sharing their children's learning in this way.
- Not all families have Internet access (we provide Internet access for parents in our setting so that they are not prevented from taking part in Starz).
- Using Starz adds to what practitioners need to do during sessions. They already run out of time needed for doing all the things they would like to be doing!
- The VLE, and adding content which means searching through files, is not totally intuitive for children and needs practitioner support.

These are clearly big challenges and need to be thought through in any setting that considers taking on a VLE. We continue to explore what these challenges mean to us and the children and families we work with. We have found some children particularly like sharing their learning in this way and the benefits have been so compelling that they outweigh the challenges. Children can plan to use a camera or movie maker specifically for communicating on their area of Starz. For example, Anat (four years old) said she was using the movie maker to take photos of her friends at Homerton so that her grandparents in Israel could see them because they would not be able to visit the setting. She was using technology for a purpose and understood that websites could be shared around the world and used for communicating. Another child, Lizzy (four years old) came into the setting and said, 'I dressed up in my bridesmaid dress. Have a look, you can see in Starz.' We logged on to her space in Starz and looked at photos of her as a bridesmaid and added our written comments for the family. Fathers, who often have greater difficulty in visiting the setting, have particularly enjoyed being able to share their children's learning through Starz.

A VLE is one way to use technology to share children's learning with families in a different and empowering way. It is by no means the only way and may be a step too far to consider for your setting at the moment. Perhaps use the ideas in Chapter 3 about using digital images to document children's learning; technology allows us to involve parents further in their children's development and achievements.

But the technology tool you choose to use to develop your communications with parents is less important than the principle itself. Select something you feel confident with – a digital camera, for example – and explore ways that you can use this more fully in your partnership with parents and carers. Most of all, enjoy the process, build your confidence using the technology, and have fun being creative with the opportunities technology can give you for developing your communications.

Appendix 1 Software and resources

Suppliers' contact details

Contact suppliers for their catalogues to see the most up-to-date list of software and resources available. Ask for thirty-day evaluations of software to try them out in your setting.

Under the suppliers' details is a list of software or resources that we have found successful for children's experiences represented in this book. Visit the publishers' websites for further details of their products.

Argos

www.argos.co.uk

- Karaoke machine
- Digital photo frames
- Metal detectors
- Channel headset walkie-talkies
- Double microphone cassette recorder

Commotion

www.commotiongroup.co.uk
Tel: 01732 773399

- Duplo remote control vehicles

Crick

www.cricksoft.com
Tel: 0845 121 1691

- Jigworks (we added our own photographs of the children or familiar objects)
- Clicker 5

Durham LEA

www.durhamlea.org.uk/publications/

- Milly's Mouse Skills

Early Learning Centre

www.elc.co.uk
Tel: 08705 352352

- Fisher Price child's camera
- Role-play and everyday technology
- Music and sound recorders and players
- Music mats

Granada Learning and SEMERC

www.granada-learning.com
Tel: 0161 827 2927

- 'At the . . .' series, including At the Doctor's, Vet's, Post Office, Garden Centre, Café and more
- Leaps and Bounds series
- Clevy keyboard (a child's keyboard)
- Children's small mice
- Tracker ball

Inclusive Technology

www.inclusive.co.uk
Tel: 01457 819790

- Choose and Tell: Nursery Rhymes
- Big Mack and other sound recorders such as Go Talk
- Bookworm

Liberator

www.pri-liberator.com
Tel: 0845 226 1144

- Talking Photo Albums
- Wide range of special needs resources
- Big Mack and other sound recorders such as the Sound Button

Logotron

www.logo.com
Tel: 01223 425558

- Revelation Natural Art

Q&D Multimedia

www.q-and-d.co.uk
Tel 01332 364963

- Beep!

Sherston

www.sherston.com
Tel: 0166 684 3200

- Tizzy's First Tools (we used Present for capturing children's stories and retelling of events using their own photographs)

Swallow Systems

www.swallow-systems.co.uk
Tel: 01494 813471

- Pixie and Pixie resources, including Pixie scribble pack

Tag Learning

www.taglearning.com
Tel: 01474 357350

- Millie's Maths House
- Some of the resources sold by other companies such as the Digital Movie Creator
- Mixman 2

2Simple

www.2simplesoftware.com
Tel: 0208 203 1781
2Simple make excellent Early Years software. This is a list of 2Simple software that we have found successful in children's experiences represented in this book:

- 2Simple Infant Video Toolkit 2
- 2Paint a Picture
- 2Simple City
- 2Maths City
- 2Create a Story
- 2Publish+
- 2Music Toolkit

TTS Group

www.tts-group.co.uk
Tel: 0800 318686

- Digital Junior Microscope (including software)
- Digital Movie Creator (including software)
- Beebots
- Bugs
- Music and sound recorders
- Talking Photo Album and Photo Cards
- Digital voice recorder
- Voice changer
- Explorer's headlamp

Visionsoft

www.childlock.com
Te: 01274 610503

- Childlock (protects files and folders on a computer from child access)

NB: We purchase adult cameras, webcams and microphones locally, so we can see and handle the resource and make sure we get exactly what we want.

Appendix 2 Ideas for using digital images

Ways of using photographs

- Record children's progress, to show their learning processes and achievements, e.g. as they build a model or complete a puzzle. Photos can track children's progress and general well-being to inform future planning.
- Communicate with parents about children's learning journeys.
- Include children in reflecting on their own learning through displays, books, etc.
- Promote children's self-esteem through showing that their play and learning are valued.
- As a learning tool, photos of familiar events can enhance learning. Children's learning can be reinforced through shared experiences recorded in video or photographs.
- If possible, take photos of the setting on home visits before they start nursery.
- Photograph special events ready for the children to take home, e.g. their birthday, their first day or special nursery day.
- Use laminated photos as a prompt, e.g. to see who is present each day.
- Take a set of photos with children to show their own life story, e.g. their family, their favourite activities, where they live.
- Reinforce your rules and routines in a positive way by photographing sharing times, children taking turns and being kind to others.
- Take sequences of photos to promote language development and story sequencing (e.g. yesterday, today and tomorrow).
- Take photos to promote specific vocabulary development such as possessive or positional language.
- Use children as characters in home-produced storyboards.
- Use photos to make letterheads, greetings cards and postcards to send home or share with others.
- Display pictures of the local environment and specific walks, e.g. a texture walk.
- Make picture-matching games with children's favourite items.
- Photograph numbers in the environment, e.g. house numbers, car number plates or signs.
- Use photos for the birthday chart.

- Use photos for PSED, e.g. feelings: matching happy faces, finding the opposite to sad, etc.
- Take spot-the-difference pictures, e.g. the book corner with and without the cushions, the sand tray with a missing sand wheel.
- Take photos of 'tools of the trade' when visitors come in, e.g. police with their bikes and nurses' or doctors' clothing.
- Take photos outdoors to show the changing seasons.
- Use photos in a slideshow for presentations at parents' evenings, open days, staff, governor or committee meetings or to show the children.
- Add photos to software for children's creative work or to recall experiences, e.g. move photos around on an interactive whiteboard to retell a cooking experience in sequence.

Appendix 3 Early Years websites

Websites for practitioners

www.standards.dcsf.gov.uk/eyfs/
www.schools.becta.org.uk
Foundation.e2bn.org
www.edu.dudley.gov.uk/foundation
ecs.lewisham.gov.uk/talent/pricor/foundation.html
www.kented.org.uk
www.northerngrid.co.uk
www.ltscotland.org.uk/earlyyears
www.ioe.ac.uk/cdl/DATEC/
ngfl.northumberland.gov.uk/ict
www.hitchams.suffolk.sch.uk/foundation
www.mape.org.uk
www.swallow.co.uk
www.publications.teachernet.gov.uk
primary-strategy.nen.gov.uk

Websites for children

www.bbc.co.uk/cbeebies
www.boowakwala.com
www.bobthebuilder.com
www.sebastianswan.org.uk
www.naturegrid.org.uk
www.bbc.co.uk/paintingtheweather
www.bbc.co.uk/schools/websites/preschool
ngfl.northumberland.gov.uk/music/orchestra
www.asiabigtime.com/storybooks
www.poissonrouge.com
www.furbies.co.uk
www.priorywoods.middlesbrough.sch.uk
www.kented.org.uk

Appendix 4 Parent questionnaire on ICT use in the home

Your help would be appreciated in completing the following questionnaire about your child's use and experience of technology in the home. The results will provide useful information in deciding on the most appropriate work to support learning about technology in the school.

No individual child or family will be identified in the survey and you can be assured of the strictest confidence.

Please complete one sheet for each child:

Age of child:_____ Sex of child: **Boy/Girl***   *Delete as required

Father's/Partner's occupation:_____

Mother's/Partner's occupation:_____

1.   Do you have a computer at home?   **Yes/No**

If the answer to Question 1 is no: fill in as much of this questionnaire as you can and put any additional comments on the back of this page.

2.   For how many hours/week does your child use it?_____

3.   Does your child operate the computer on their own?   **Yes/No**

4.   What programs do they normally use? (Please list these by name on the back of this page . . .)

Also does your child possess any electronic toys, e.g. a Furby, Techno Robotic Puppy, etc. (Again please name these overleaf . . .)

5.   Please complete the following table, using ticks to indicate how often:

As a parent I:	Never	Sometimes	Weekly	Daily
Read with my child				
Take my child to the library				
Sing songs and rhymes with my child				
Spend time with my child on the computer				
Teach numbers and alphabet				

6.   At what age do you think children should be introduced to computers:

At home:_____   At school:_____

Why?

Thank you for your time: Please add any further comments that you may wish to make on the subject of early computer experience on the reverse of the sheet. Then pass the questionnaire to any member of staff so that it can be returned to us for analysis.

Appendix 5 Ideas for using the digital movie maker

Children could:

- Use the camera attached to the computer as well as unattached. It can be easier for children to record when the video is attached, as they don't have to keep the button depressed.
- See themselves and each other through the monitor, use the camera as a 'television'.
- Use the camera in role play, both freely as part of a home or holiday environment and to film their own role play while they put stories together.
- Use the camera to record events, outings, etc. These will be very different when recorded by children. What did they choose to film? Put together videos from different children into a 'movie' as a way of sharing different viewpoints and interests.
- Collect evidence for a shared interest, e.g. mini-beasts.
- Take the camera home to record a weekend or a specific time they want to share with the setting, e.g. they could go home with a bear and the bear's weekend could be recorded.

Practitioners could:

- Take a range of both moving and still images for planning for development, e.g. take video of one area over a period of time and use this for observation and planning changes.
- Share video with parents or for training purposes.
- Make video of children retelling stories and use it as a 'library' with the children for inspiring storytelling.
- Take video footage of children engaged in role play. Show it back through the computer screen or through a Smart Board and encourage children to retell their experiences or look for opportunities to build on next steps.
- Take video footage of children engaged in role play and make it into talking books using PowerPoint or Smart Board software.
- Use stop motion animation to record children constructing.
- Work in partnership with the children to create a video for a specific purpose, e.g.

put together children in a number line in an imaginative way where they are the actors and can be teaching those who watch to count from 1 to 10.

- Use for backdrops with an overhead projector and a screen or an interactive white-board, either for puppet shows or with film taken from another environment to support role play.
- Take video of events, outings, etc. and use it to support language development. Put together videos from different children into a 'movie' as a way of sharing different viewpoints and interests.

Hot tip

You can use the self-timer as a way of helping children who can't keep the video record button depressed.

Using the self-timer on the camera

- Push and release the 'Self-timer' button. The timer icon on the LCD will turn on and begin to blink.
- Push the 'Video' button if you want to capture a video.
- A ticking sound will play before the video begins to record. When the sound stops, a final sound will play, signalling that the camera is about to begin recording the video.
- The camera will continue to record a video until either all the memory is used up or you push any other button on the camera to stop the recording.

Appendix 6 Observing, planning, assessing: how can technology help us?

Use ICT to help you make and communicate your observations

- Take close-up photographs of children to record their learning and achievements. Does the picture tell a story?
- Display photographs for parents and carers to celebrate children's learning; instead of a single photo of an activity, try taking a series and making a montage, perhaps zooming in on children's hands or the materials they are using.
- Use a computer/laptop/IWB/plasma screen to display slideshows of photographs of children's playful learning. If you do not have a computer you can buy digital photo frames that display a slideshow of photographs.
- Record a learning journey with photographs. Share these with the children and their families by putting them into books or on a display.
- Not all photos need to be printed. Share children's experiences with them by looking through the play-back feature of the camera. This is also a good way to share your observations quickly and immediately with parents and carers, e.g. when a child is settling into the nursery.
- Use digital video to observe learning and share with small groups of children through a computer screen or IWB, e.g. children will notice experiences like jumping in puddles, or seeing shadows, in different ways when they reflect back on the experience.
- If you capture audio digitally, think how you will use this. Try to save time by keeping it in digital form and not transcribing it. Perhaps it could be added to a child's digital portfolio, or added to a PowerPoint sharing children's learning.

Use ICT to help with planning

- Make sure you have proformas ready on a computer for all types of planning: long, medium and short term and for planned focused experiences.
- Use the electronic version of the Early Years Foundation Stage (PDF document) so that you can cut and paste next steps into your planning.
- Used planning documents can be stored on the computer and adapted for use with other groups of children. Try to avoid creating everything from scratch.

- Show children photographs and video of themselves at play through slideshows on a computer screen, IWB, plasma screen or digital photo frame. They will look back on what they were doing and often this will spark their own planning to continue with the experience.
- Use books and PowerPoint 'talking books' to share children's learning journeys with them. This can encourage shared planning for future experiences.
- Use photos and video from the local environment, e.g. a garden centre, to help plan role-play scenarios with the children and involve their families.

Use ICT to help you make and communicate your assessments

- Encourage children to photograph their own learning and achievements and to put them into a book or into a folder on the computer. Help them add captions. Help them become reflective learners.
- Build a digital portfolio of children's achievements. This could be online and built up with parents and carers through a virtual learning environment.
- Digital audio could easily be added to the above and will help involve children in making statements about their personal learning experience.
- Use photos in assessments shared with parents, carers and other professionals. Develop your skill in taking photographs that communicate children's achievements well. A digital camera is ideal for this because you can take many photos and only actually use one.
- Use digital video for children to make their own record of achievements. This need not be expensive: a webcam works well here.

Appendix 7 Needs audit: EYFS ICT baseline skills and knowledge

From: Price, Harriet (ed.), *The Really Useful Book of ICT in the Early Years*, London: Routledge, © Harriet Price 2009.

Area of knowledge or skill	Date of training	Delivered by	Practised	Need for further training/support	Incorporated into practice
Planning for ICT in the Foundation Stage					
Organise ICT within the setting					
Plan activities using ICT across all areas of learning					
Use ICT to support creative development					
Use technology in role play					
Skills and knowledge for children					
To be able to give instruction in new applications in response to children's interests or needs and to teach the skills associated with launching and navigating programs					
To be able to take a small group, or individuals, through software or hardware, using appropriate vocabulary and encouraging children to talk about their use of technology					
Laptop/Desktop skills for yourself					
Familiarity with opening, creating and saving files (including to a USB memory stick)					
To be able to switch between Windows and copy, paste, transfer or delete files from a folder					
To be able to import and manipulate images					
To be able to select appropriate printer settings					
To be able to find and launch programs					
To be able to create and delete shortcuts					
To be able to set up a working desktop for young children					
To be able to set up hyperlinks to websites enabling children to select choices through icons					
Software skills					
To be able to use Microsoft Word for word processing					
To be able to use PowerPoint for creating a slideshow, or to be able to use slideshow software (such as that provided in Windows XP) to show a sequence of pictures					
To have a knowledge of and be able to use software that supports early learning, including children with special needs					
To be able to use software that comes with peripheral devices, e.g. a digital camera					
Peripherals					
To be able to take, download and print pictures with a digital camera					
To be able to use a programmable toy for learning and teaching					
To be able to operate other peripherals you might have access to, e.g. a scanner, a digital microscope, a webcam or an interactive whiteboard					
Communication					
To be able to access the Internet and use email					
To be able to support children in using websites and sending email cards					

Appendix 8 Guidance on observing and assessing ICT

The Early Years Foundation Stage profile

The profile is a way of summing up each child's progress at the end of the foundation stage. It is based on ongoing observations and assessments in all six areas of Learning and Development. ICT is specifically mentioned in Knowledge and Understanding, and the Early Learning Goal states that children should be able to:

*   Complete a simple program on a computer.
*   Use ICT to perform simple functions, such as selecting a channel on the TV remote control.
*   Use a mouse and keyboard to interact with age-appropriate computer software.
*   Find out about and identify the uses of everyday technology and use Information and Communications Technology and programmable toys to support their learning.

This much will be recorded within the profile, but ICT is a learning tool and there are opportunities across all areas of development as reflected in the Early Years Foundation Stage planning document. Young children are ever more technologically aware and new resources are enabling children to access ICT tools at an increasingly young age. They are now transferring to new settings with a surprising degree of ICT knowledge and skills and some practitioners are looking for ways to observe and assess children's ICT capability across areas of learning. This helps inform their own practice and enables them to pass on useful information about children's achievements.

Observation and assessment

Practitioners make judgments about children's progress through observing children; interacting with them, using well-thought-out questions and listening and talking. Any assessment of ICT needs to be seen in this context.

It's not necessary to assess discrete skills because the skills will show through observation of whole tasks – for example, if a child is able to use a paint program we know they are also able to use a mouse competently, able to make choices, select colours, use certain tools and possibly print or save their work.

Children will demonstrate ICT capability as they interact with their peers, their environment and the adults in the setting. Brief notes within your observations will be very useful in building a picture of a child's ICT capability.

A quick reminder: ICT is not just about computer use, or just about achieving skills. It includes children's growing technological awareness, their understanding that there are ICT tools that they can experiment with and find out about, that they can begin to control and can use for their own purposes.

Questions that might help inform your observations of children using ICT

- Are they interested in and curious about technology? Do they enter into discussion and make comments?
- Do they experiment with ICT applications, finding things out for themselves?
- Do they show enjoyment and concentration?
- Are they able to use ICT for their own purposes, e.g. use a tape recorder to hear a story or a metal detector to find treasure?
- Do they incorporate ICT into their role play and demonstrate an understanding of its purposes?
- Do they talk about ICT tools and applications and show an understanding of their purposes?
- Are they able to find and start a program?
- Are they able to navigate a program?
- Are they beginning to experiment with tapping out letters using the keyboard?
- Are they showing an awareness of electronic forms of communication, email, Internet, mobile texts?
- Do they know, are they able to find out, what buttons and icons do?
- Do they print or save their pictures?
- Are they able to insert a tape and press the 'Play' and 'Eject' buttons?
- Are they able to control a toy and make it move where they want?

Questions that might prompt discussion with children in the context of their play

- What happened?
- What can it do?
- How do we make it work?
- What do people use these for?
- I wonder what this button will do?
- What else do you like to use a computer/tape recorder/camera for?
- What will happen if . . .?
- Have you had a go on the computer/tape recorder/camera? What did you do?

Appendix 9 ICT and individual needs: a directory

ICT is particularly enabling for children with Special Educational Needs; it can provide access to experiences that might be hard for some children to access through any other means and thereby aids children's development.

It is also highly motivating, can help build children's confidence in their abilities and is an excellent focus for social interaction.

Some children in your setting may have learning difficulties caused by any number of reasons from a physical disability to emotional difficulties or a medical condition. The use of ICT can be essential in enabling all children to gain access to the curriculum.

For children with physical and sensory disabilities, using ICT can

- Enable children to be included in experiences alongside their peer group, allowing their learning to take place within a social context
- Provide switch or adapted access to tape recorder, computer, moving toys, etc. and thereby to playful learning experiences
- Produce outcomes that can be on a par with their peer group, e.g. a printout from a paint program
- Provide alternative means of communication and translate text into speech and speech into text
- Aid adults in preparing materials which are specially adapted with large pictures, fonts, symbols and particular colours
- Give children a level of independence.

For pupils with learning difficulties, using ICT can

- Offer a medium for differentiated experiences
- Enable children to repeatedly practise and reinforce skills and understandings in different contexts
- Enhance the development of activities that are clear, focused and motivating to children
- Support language development and offer multi-sensory ways of learning.

For pupils with emotional and behavioural difficulties, using ICT can

- offer children a non-threatening or non-judgmental situation;
- be motivating and offer opportunities for success;
- enable independent learning;
- encourage children to cooperate with an adult or someone in their peer group;
- aid adults in preparing materials that support children in managing things that they find difficult, e.g. using picture symbols to timetable activities, events or their day.

Hardware resources for children with special needs

Children with special needs in Early Years settings will often be able to use the same ICT equipment as their peer group. For many children in the Early Years this will be enough to support their development. Sometimes they may need more specialist equipment to allow them access to experiences: switches/switch control box, keyboards with large clear buttons, tracker balls, joysticks, communication aids. Sometimes technology such as sensory equipment can offer enhanced experiences to children with special needs.

Specialist equipment may enable children to use a computer, switch toys on and off or aid communication. Finding the right access can be a bit of a minefield and may require specialist help such as an occupational therapist. Publishing companies themselves can be very helpful and are worth phoning for information.

Companies that will send out a catalogue and sell specialist equipment

Crick Software
01604 671691

Widgit Software
01223 425558

SEMERC
0845 602 1937

Inclusive Technology
01457 819790

Keytools
0238 058 4314

Liberator
0845 226 1144

Software for children with special needs

Again there is plenty of software that children with special needs will benefit from alongside their peer group; look at Leaps and Bounds, for example, for developing language and an understanding of cause and effect.

Some software is developmental and aims to teach a child that from this simple cause and effect level they can move on to deciding for themselves what will happen next, they can make choices, plan actions and predict outcomes.

Examples of these are: Microworlds, Sequences and Face Paint 2 (available from SEMERC along with Leaps and Bounds). They are appropriate for all young children, but particularly for those with special needs, because of their bright screens, clear buttons and the way they have been designed to be used with an adult to encourage language development.

There is some specialist software, for example Switch Software. This usually operates on a simple cause and effect level and encourages children to gain a sense that they have some control over the equipment. Examples of these are Touch games 1 and 2. These and many others are available from SEMERC or Inclusive Technology.

Other specialist software includes Writing with Symbols, Boardmaker or Communicate in Print (Widgit), which can be used to support communication and is usually used by adults to make resources for children in the Foundation Stage.

Clicker 5 supports communicating by using pictures, speech and words. These companies can be contacted through the phone numbers above.

Appendix 10 Guidance on monitoring ICT

Why monitor?

- Is it possible that the children who come to the setting with the most ICT skills and understanding also leave with the most? Are we able to bridge that divide at all?
- How do we recognise what stage children are at with ICT and know what to provide next to support, encourage and enable them?
- How do we know that we are engaging girls as well as boys? All our cultures? Including individual needs and challenging the more able?
- Are we considering dialogue with parents and professionals and transfer of children from one setting to another?

What is it that we could purposefully and usefully monitor?

- children's growing awareness of the technological world;
- ICT skills, understanding and progress;
- children's ability to access and use equipment.

The recording of this monitoring needs to be useful for planning and for parents, other professionals and for transfer to the next setting.

How to monitor individuals and groups

- Keep within the ways that you are already evaluating.
- Try to resist tick lists of discrete skills. If a child can paint and print a copy of their work on the computer, they can adequately use a mouse, know what icons are and can find a button to send to print. A detailed one-minute observation of the child using a piece of ICT equipment might tell you much more.
- Plan to quickly observe all the children two or three times a year to see if and how they are accessing equipment and what their next steps might be.
- Plan to quickly monitor access by groups of children, e.g. are girls accessing the computer as often as the boys? For different programs?

- What about a folder for each child, or a group of children, on the computer? You could add their achievements over the year, e.g. an electronic painting, digital photographs, scanned work, etc. This folder could also help you and the children's families celebrate the children's technological achievements over their time in your setting.

Appendix 11 Example photograph permission form

Photograph/video permission form

I am the parent/legal guardian of the child named below and I give permission for my child to be photographed or videotaped whilst in the care of the setting for the following purposes (please tick all that apply);

- Setting only – this may include

    - Photo albums
    - Displays
    - Staff coursework

- Training other professionals
- Printed media
- Internet

Child's name [block capitals]

Parent's name [block capitals]

Class

Parent signature(s) **Date**

FOR CHILD PROTECTION REASONS, CHILDREN'S NAMES WILL NOT BE GIVEN IN ANY PUBLICATION

From: Price, Harriet (ed.), *The Really Useful Book of ICT in the Early Years*, London: Routledge, © Harriet Price 2009.

Appendix 12 Planning for ICT through a thematic approach

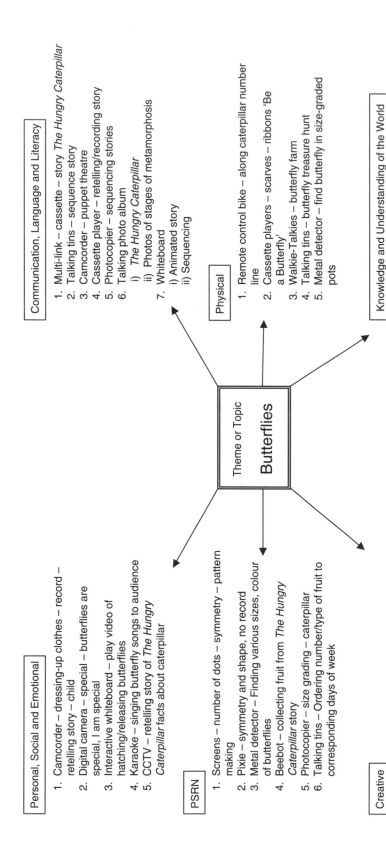

Theme or Topic
Butterflies

Communication, Language and Literacy

1. Multi-link – cassette – story *The Hungry Caterpillar*
2. Talking tins – sequence story
3. Camcorder – puppet theatre
4. Cassette player – retelling/recording story
5. Photocopier – sequencing stories
6. Talking photo album
   i) *The Hungry Caterpillar*
   ii) Photos of stages of metamorphosis
7. Whiteboard
   i) Animated story
   ii) Sequencing

Physical

1. Remote control bike – along caterpillar number line
2. Cassette players – scarves – ribbons 'Be a Butterfly'
3. Walkie-Talkies – butterfly farm
4. Talking tins – butterfly treasure hunt
5. Metal detector – find butterfly in size-graded pots

Knowledge and Understanding of the World

1. Pixie – Life-cycle – collecting items in order – collecting fruit, fruits to test and taste
2. Talking tins – sequence – butterfly farm
3. Webcam – hatching – butterflies
4. Microwave – smoothie maker – fruits from story
5. Bread maker – change

Personal, Social and Emotional

1. Camcorder – dressing-up clothes – record – retelling story – child
2. Digital camera – special – butterflies are special, I am special
3. Interactive whiteboard – play video of hatching/releasing butterflies
4. Karaoke – singing butterfly songs to audience
5. CCTV – retelling story of *The Hungry Caterpillar* facts about caterpillar

PSRN

1. Screens – number of dots – symmetry – pattern making
2. Pixie – symmetry and shape, no record
3. Metal detector – Finding various sizes, colour of butterflies
4. Beebot – collecting fruit from *The Hungry Caterpillar* story
5. Photocopier – size grading – caterpillar
6. Talking tins – Ordering number/type of fruit to corresponding days of week

Creative

1. OHP – silhouettes of butterflies in garden
2. Digital microscope – looking at wings, etc. – draw – create pattern using colour and texture
3. Webcam – animation – butterfly
4. Scanner or digital camera –draw butterfly and make into jigsaw

Appendix 13 Medium-term planning sheet: all areas of learning

MEDIUM-TERM PLANNING	EARLY LEARNING GOAL	DATE STEPS FOR LEARNING	RESOURCES/EVENTS
PERSONAL/SOCIAL EMOTIONAL DEVELOPMENT	➤ Able to treat living things, property and environment with care, concern and respect ➤ Responds appropriately to the Easter story	Wk 1: Shows care and concern for living things Wk 2: Gains an understanding and insight into the celebration of St David's Day Wk 3: Using Red Nose Day as a stimulus – becomes aware that there are people less fortunate than ourselves Wk 4: Shows care and concern for indoor/outdoor environment – gains an insight into Mothering Sunday Wk 5: Listens to and responds to significant events in the Easter story	Shrove Tuesday – 20th February Red Nose Day – St David's Day – 1st March St Patrick's Day – 17th March Mothering Sunday – 18th March Easter –
COMMUNICATION, LANGUAGE AND LITERACY Listening Speaking Reading Writing	➤ Enjoys listening to and using spoken and written language ➤ Uses pictures and symbols to communicate meaning	Wk 1: Listens to core story in a group with and without focus object Wk 2: Describes main story settings, events and principal characters Wk 3: Listens to taped story, self on tape and listens to other children in group Wk 4: Records/retells story of core book, using pictures and simple text Wk 5: Uses pictures and symbols to communicate meaning – cards – symbols of Easter story, cup, bread, wine, cross	**Core Books** *Farmer Duck* *Little Lumpty* *Are You My Mother?*
PSRN	➤ Talks about, recognises and recreates simple patterns ➤ Shows awareness of symmetry	Wk 1: Understands that patterns can be repeated and copies a simple line pattern Wk 2: Talks about and explores simple patterns in the environment and makes own pattern (2 attributes) Wk 3: Able to pattern and sequence using 3 attributes Wk 4: Shows an awareness of symmetry Wk 5: Shows an awareness/understanding of tessellation and uses shapes to tessellate	**Shop** Pet shop Walks in environment Peg boards Logi-blocks Tiler-computer Camera Beads Mirrors

Area	Learning objectives	Weekly activities	Resources
KNOWLEDGE AND UNDERSTANDING OF THE WORLD CDT Science History Geography ICT	➢ Finds out about and identifies some features of living things and gains an understanding of life-cycles ➢ Explores and constructs a range of products through the skills of cutting and tearing	Wk 1: Understands the growth cycle of a plant and represents this pictorially Wk 2: Understands the life-cycle of a chicken and talks about and names other farm animals Wk 3: Understands and recalls the various stages of metamorphosis associated with frogs Wk 4: Develops cutting and tearing skills through work on life-cycles Wk 5: Develops cutting and tearing skills, using a variety of materials to make Easter crafts	Incubator and fertilised eggs Frog spawn Growing seeds and bulbs Life-cycle jigsaws Sequencing cards Digital camera
PHYSICAL DEVELOPMENT Ball play/skills Wheeled toys Natural Agility	➢ Understands the concept of 'push' and 'pull' ➢ Handles tools, objects, construction and malleable materials safely and with increasing control	Wk 1: Develops co-ordination needed to push and pedal toys such as scooters and tricycles Wk 2: Develops co-ordination to control digging, brushing, weeding/ Understands that equipment and tools have to be used safely Wk 3: Builds, using large construction play outdoors Wk 4: Develops co-ordination skills to control different sizes of balls for patting, rolling pushing, kicking Wk 5: Develop co-ordination skills to push, pedal and pull outdoor toys, to dig, throw, catch, aim roll, etc.	Pushing/pulling toys Rope tug of war Construction toys Woodwork bench, tools, nails, wood
CREATIVE DEVELOPMENT Art and Craft Music and Dance	➢ Represents animals and plants through observational paintings, drawings, models and collage ➢ Responds creatively to the stimuli of Easter ➢ Responds to symbols for hard/soft – fast/ slow – stop/start	Wk 1: Observational paintings, pictures, drawings and collage of plants, flowers, seeds and bulbs – to be able to reproduce Wk 2: Observational paintings, pictures, drawings, collage models of farm animals Wk 3: To gain an understanding of the colour 'red' and produce a variety of 'red' art work Wk 4: To respond creatively to the stimuli of Mothering Sunday, St Patrick's Day and Easter Wk 5: To respond creatively to the stimuli of Easter	Plants, animals, flowers Brushes of various sizes Observational paintings of local area for art exhibition Egg marbling

Appendix 14 Weekly planning sheet: all areas of learning

Area	Monday	Tuesday	Wednesday	Thursday	Friday
PSRN objective Talks about and explores simple patterns in the environment and makes own pattern (2 attributes)					
Table I	Printing wall using two colours – ink; Observing photos wall	Picture lotto – shape; Pattern in environment – make own pattern and record	Look at patterns on animals – record animal pattern	Looking at patterns on wrapping paper	Pattern walk in the environment; Digital photographs/lotto game ●□
Small construction	Rhythm et Persles	Tizzy's Box – Duplo	ASCO	Clic	Wooden bricks
Computer/ICT	My World Beads	My World Building Bricks	Dazzle	My World – stripes and spots – zebra – giraffe	1,2,3 – number sequences
Shop	Pet shop →				
Creative objective Observational paintings, pictures, drawings, collage, models of farm animals					
Table I	Paintings of cows/pigs	Observational paintings of chickens; Laptop/video	Overhead projector; Life-size paintings	Clay models of farm animals; Laptop pictures of farm animals	Collage of pigs; Different shades pink paper
Table 2	Laptop; Farm animals	Green paper – black felt pens – chalk	Junk models of farm animals	Observational pencil drawings	Texture pictures
Easel	Observational drawings – pastels	Observational drawings of chicks	Charcoal	Free painting	Free painting
Communication, Language and Literacy objective Describes main story settings, events and principal characters					
Table I	Draw scene from *Farmer Duck* – label using initial sounds – emergent writing ●	Talking tins – characters from *Farmer Duck* – feelings/characteristics	Recap – matching main characters to setting; Photocopied images	*Little Lumpty* – night-time scene – place and character + setting; Webcam animation ●	Story line – events of *Are You My Mother?* ●
Writing table	Zig zag non-fiction book	Letter of week 'c'	Kim's Game 'c'	Tracking – Lumpty to wall, etc.	Handwriting – anti clockwise patterns for 'e' ●
Book corner	Animal jigsaws	Multi-link *Farmer Duck*	Puppet theatre	Animal lotto	Adult reading session
Small world	Farm Scene	Train track and wooden farm animals	Zoo	Castle	Dinosaurs
Home corner	Washing and cleaning →				
Computer	Brown Bear on Farm	My World	ABC	Oxford Reading Tree □	Internet
Jigsaws	Farmer Duck	Insect puzzles	Animal puzzles	Healthy Food	Animal puzzles

	Thursday	Friday	Monday	Tuesday	Wednesday
Personal, Social and Emotional objective — Gains an understanding and insight into St David's Day Show care and concern for living things △	Listen to explanation about St David's Day – look at artefacts – sheep/daffodil, castle. Video	Talk about St David's Day. Fantasy story about dragon. Interview using CCTV. ○	Discussion about what animals need to stay healthy ○	Objects from pet shop. What is it? Who needs it? What is it for? Talking tins ○	Dog puppet. Talking about what makes him happy/sad ○
Physical objective — Develops co-ordination to control digging, brushing, weeding. Understands that tools have to be used safely △ — **Outside**	Tidying sensory garden. Tape recorder ●□	Simon Says . . . sweep the floor, dig the garden ●□	Planting and digging ●●□	Obstacle course/garden. Digital stop watch □○	Pushing/pulling. Wheelbarrows ○
Verandah	Train track/climbing frame □	ASCO / Climbing Frame □	Castle/sliding □	Wooden bricks. Sliding and swinging □	Garage and vehicles. Jumping. Balancing □
Knowledge and Understanding of the World objective — Understands the life-cycle of a chicken and talks about and names other farm animals △ — **Table I**	Introduce non-fiction books *Finding out about Farm Animals*. Laptop/ video about farm animals	Make a simple farm book. Talking tins to record animal sounds	Life-cycle of chicken. Pixie. Record pictorially	Metal detector. Pictures of farm animals. Find – name/animal sounds	Non-fiction life-cycle book. Life-cycle (split pin)
Sand	Diggers and trucks	Buckets and spades	Dinosaurs	Animal sand moulds	Plant pots and scoops
Water	Water wheels – jugs	Boat and play people	Funnels and jugs	Cornflour and sieves	Bubbles and dolls
Malleable	Goop	Spaghetti	Play dough chickens	Play dough	Rice and micro-instruments
Music/movement	Dance □△	Instruments △	Sticks △	Dance in large hall □△	Large group singing △
Book focus		*Are You My Mother?*	*Little Lumpty*	*Farmer Duck*	
Weekly Rhyme		'5 Eggs and 5 Eggs'	'Old McDonald'		

Special events/visitors/other activities

□ Be healthy
△ Enjoy and achieve
● Stay safe
○ Make a positive contribution
▲ Achieve economic well-being

Appendix 15 Weekly planning sheet: Knowledge and Understanding of the World

Understands the life-cycle of a chicken and talks about and names other farm animals		*Short-term planning*		*Date:*	
	Activity	*Learning intention (differentiation)*		*Adult input questions and vocabulary*	*Evaluation*
		Knowledge	*Skill*		
Thursday	Introduce non-fiction books *Finding Out About Farm Animals* Internet farm website	1. Looks at books with interest 2. Can name some of the animals 3. Can name animals and asks and answers questions about animals	Reference Discussion Questioning Listening	Non-fiction Information Fact Cow, pig, sheep, horse, ducks, chickens, etc.	
Friday	Make simple farm books Talking tins to record animal sounds	1. Makes book with adult support 2. Can make corresponding animal sounds 3. Represents and attempts writing in books	Representation Emergent writing ICT – recording and playing	What sound/noise does a cow make?, etc. Can you draw a cow? Now let's find the sound . . .	
Monday	Life-cycle of a chicken Pixie Record pictorially	1. Can complete life-cycle with support 2. Can complete life-cycle independently 3. Records life-cycle of a chicken	Sequencing Observation Discussion Recording ICT – programming Pixie	Egg Pixie Hatch Forward Chick Backwards Chicken Numbers Lay	
Tuesday	Metal detector Pictures of farm animals	1. Can name a farm animal 2. Can name all pictures of farm animals 3. Can name and match animal sounds with confidence	Recall Observation Matching Discussion ICT – metal detector	What have you found? How do you know you have found something? Animal names Animal sounds	
Wednesday	Non-fiction life-cycle book/non-fiction life-cycle using split pins My World screen-reinforcement of life-cycle	1. Represents life-cycle with support 2. Represents life-cycle independently 3. Asks and answers questions about life-cycles	Reference Representation Discussion Questioning Technology – joining	Egg Nest Chicken Chick Hatch Lay Farm	

Appendix 16 Medium-term planning sheet: ICT

Early Learning Goal: To develop ICT competency and to use programmable toys to support learning

Week	Development matters	Activities (learning opportunities/levels of differentiation)	Play opportunities	Resources
1.	Knows how to operate simple equipment	1. Help children to become aware of technology in nursery setting 2. To develop simple skills of using equipment – on/off button 3. Control programmable toys	Tape Karaoke machine Two-way telephones CCTV Bread-making machine	Barcode scanner Electronic till Metal detector Tape recorder Overhead projector
2.	Follows instructions to use a digital camera	1. Familiarise children with use and care of camera 2. Introduce/use language associated with camera 3. Begin to differentiate process of taking photographs	Use of real and play cameras Photostudio	Old cameras Pretend cameras Digital cameras Camcorder
3.	Understands the purpose of simple controls	1. Able to use on/off buttons on tape recorders, handsets, cameras cars, etc. 2. Uses play and stop buttons 3. Able to rewind/ forward/skip track on cassette and CD player	Tape recorders in story corner (multi-link) and in house Karaoke machine/ stage	Remote control cars Pixie Programmable toys Cameras Metal detector
4.	Able to respond to a variety of computer programs	1. Uses computer 2. Completes simple programs with help 3. Begins to differentiate process of using computer – moves mouse/moves mouse and clicks/ moves mouse and clicks, drags, drops	Specially made My World Screens Interactive screens Talking books ORT books Bailey's Book House, etc.	Sherston Programs 2Easy Millie's Maths, etc.
5.	Understands and uses correct technological language	1. Is introduced to language of everyday equipment – television, video, microwave, etc. 2. Use correct language associated with computer hardware 3. Use language associated with peripherals	Technological equipment in home corner, shop area and imaginative play area – changed each half-term	Photocopier Television Computer Video Remote control Scanner

Week	Development matters	Activities (learning opportunities/levels of differentiation)	Play opportunities	Resources
6.	Uses ICT in role-play situation	1. Till, barcode scanner in shop, video and television 2. Cameras in all areas of the nursery 3. Bread-making machine, microwave, pasta maker, washing machine 4. Remote control toys 5. CCTV link between verandah and home play area 6. Telephone links between house and shop		Bread maker Remote control cars Programmable toys Metal detectors Walkie-talkies CD player

Bibliography

Adams, A. and Brindley, S., 'Series Editors Preface' in M. Hayes and D. Whitebread (eds) (2006) *ICT in the Early Years* (Maidenhead: Open University Press).

Bermudez, A.B., Rakow, S.J. and Ensle, A.L. (eds) (1992) *Critical Issues in Parental Involvement: A Collection of Research Summaries by Title VII Graduate Students* (Washington: ERIC Project).

Bilton, H., James, K., Wilson, A. and Woonton, M. (eds) (2005) *Learning Outdoors: Improving the Quality of Young Children's Play Outdoors* (London: David Fulton).

Coia, L. and Taylor, M. (2001) *Future Perfect: Reflecting through Personal Narrative* (Washington: ERIC Project).

Crook, cited in *Early Learning in the Knowledge Society: Report on a European Conference*, 22–23 May 2003 (Brussels: International Business Machines).

Edwards, C., Gandini, L. and Forman, G. (eds) (1993) *The Hundred Languages of Children: The Reggio Emilia Approach to Early Childhood Education* (Norwood, NJ: Ablex).

Feasey, R., Gair, J. and Shaw, P. (2003) *Evaluation of the Intel Play QX3 Microscope* (London: Report to BECTA).

Fine, C. and Thornbury, M.L. (2006) 'ICT: Play and Exploration' in Hayes and Whitebread (eds) *ICT in the Early Years* (Maidenhead: Open University Press).

Lancaster, P. (2003) *Listening to Young Children* (Maidenhead: Open University Press).

Marsh, J. (2006) 'Digital Animation in the Early Years: ICT and Media Education', in Hayes and Whitebread (eds), *ICT in the Early Years* (Maidenhead: Open University Press).

Northamptonshire County Council (2003) *Transforming Teaching and Learning through ICT in Schools*.

QCA (2000) *Curriculum Guidance for the Foundation Stage* (London: HMSO).

Siraj-Blatchford, I. and Siraj-Blatchford, J. (2003) *More than Computers: Information and Communications Technology in the Early Years* (London: British Association for Early Childhood Education).

Siraj-Blatchford, I. and Siraj-Blatchford, J. (2006a) *A Guide to Developing the ICT Curriculum for Early Childhood Education* (Stoke on Trent: Trentham Books).

Siraj-Blatchford, I. and Siraj-Blatchford, J. (2006b) 'Towards a Future Early Years Curriculum' in Hays and Whitebread (eds), *ICT in the Early Years* (Maidenhead: Open University Press).

Siraj-Blatchford, I., Sylva, K., Muttock, S. and Gilden, R. (2002) *Effective Pedagogy in the Early Years* (London: DfES Research Report 356).

Siraj-Blatchford, J. and Whitebread, D. (2003) *Supporting ICT in the Early Years* (Maidenhead: Open University Press).

Trythall, A. *The Little Book of ICT: Little Books with Big Ideas* (Husbands Bosworth: Featherstone Education Ltd).

Whitebread, D. (2007) 'Developing Independence in Learning' in J. Moyles (ed.) *Challenges and Issues in Early Childhood* (Maidenhead: Open University Press).

Online

EYFS (DCSF 2007)
www.standards.dcsf.gov.uk/eyfs/

Madden, L. (2002) Calculating the digital divide
www.spiked-online.com/Printable/00000006D86D.htm

Guldberg, H. (2002) From ABC to ICT
www.spiked-online.com/Articles/00000002D442.htm

Ofsted (2005) Every Child Matters: framework for the inspection of schools in England. London: HMI
www.ofsted.gov.uk

Prensky, M. (2001) Digital natives digital immigrants
pre2005.flexiblelearning.net.au/projects/resources/Digital_Natives_Digital_Immigrants.pdf

McPake, J., Stephen, C., Plowman, L., Sime, D. and Downey, S. Already at a disadvantage? ICT in the home and children's preparation for primary school. Institute of Education, University of Stirling 2005
www.ioe.stir.ac.uk/research/projects/interplay/docs/already_at_a_disadvantage.pdf

UNICEF (1991) Children's rights and responsibilities: a summary of the United Nations Convention on the Rights of the Child.
www.unicef.org.uk

Children in Europe. Issue 8. Space to play, room to grow. Matti Bergstrom and Pia Ikonen.
www.childreninscotland.org.uk/cie

Early learning, forward thinking: spreading the word
www.ltscotland.org.uk

Learning through landscapes: Early Years vision and values for outdoor play
www.standards.dcsf.gov.uk/eyfs/resources/downloads/vision-and-values-sign-up.pdf

Index